Puppy Training Bible
6 Simple Steps

Positive Reinforcement for Busy Owners to Potty Train, Master Basic Commands, Apply 10-Minute Lessons, Curb Bad Habits & Raise a Confident Dog at All Ages

TRINITY WOODS
PRESS

Copyright © Trinity Woods Press 2025 - All rights reserved.

The content contained within this book may not be reproduced, duplicated or transmitted without direct written permission from the author or the publisher.

Under no circumstances will any blame or legal responsibility be held against the publisher, or author, for any damages, reparation, or monetary loss due to the information contained within this book. Either directly or indirectly. You are responsible for your own choices, actions, and results.

Legal Notice:

This book is copyright protected. This book is only for personal use. You cannot amend, distribute, sell, use, quote or paraphrase any part, or the content within this book, without the consent of the author or publisher.

Disclaimer Notice:

Please note the information contained within this document is for educational and entertainment purposes only. All effort has been executed to present accurate, up to date, and reliable, complete information. No warranties of any kind are declared or implied. Readers acknowledge that the author is not engaging in the rendering of legal, financial, medical or professional advice. The content within this book has been derived from various sources. Please consult a licensed professional before attempting any techniques outlined in this book.

By reading this document, the reader agrees that under no circumstances is the author responsible for any losses, direct or indirect, which are incurred as a result of the use of the information contained within this document, including, but not limited to, — errors, omissions, or inaccuracies.

Book Cover by Trinity Woods Press. Illustrations by Trinity Woods Press

1st edition 2025

"The righteous care for the needs of their animals."
Proverbs 12:10 (NIV)

Dedicated to every dog lover that chooses patience over punishment, connection over control, and love over frustration- this journey is for you.

I hope the time you invest brings out the very best in your dog, and deepens the bond you share.

— Trinity Woods Press

Contents

Introduction	9
1. PREPARING FOR YOUR PUPPY'S ARRIVAL	13
Crafting Your Puppy Supply Checklist	14
Puppy-Proofing Your Home for Safety	16
Setting Up a Stress-Free Crate Space	18
Scheduling Your First Vet Visit	21
2. BRINGING YOUR PUPPY HOME	23
Creating a First-Day Routine for Success	26
Building Initial Trust and Bonding	28
Minimizing Separation Anxiety from Day One	29
Bonus Section: Naming Your New Puppy	31
Teaching Your Puppy Their Name	33
3. STEP ONE: POTTY TRAINING	35
Recognizing Your Puppy's Potty Cues	38
Troubleshooting Common Potty Training Issues	39
Using Potty Pads and Outdoor Training Techniques	41
4. STEP TWO: CRATE TRAINING	44
Introducing Your Puppy to the Crate	46
Making the Crate a Positive Space	48
Gradual Crate Training for Success	50
5. STEP THREE: PREVENTING FOOD AGGRESSION	53
Implementing Safe Feeding Practices	55
Addressing and Correcting Food Guarding	58
Teaching "Leave It" and "Wait" Commands	60

6. STEP FOUR: SOCIALIZING YOUR PUPPY — 65
   Introducing Your Puppy to New People and Pets — 68
   Navigating Public Spaces with Confidence — 70
   Managing Overexcitement and Fear — 72

7. STEP FIVE: TEACHING RECALL — 75
   Positive Reinforcement for Recall Success — 78
   Practicing Recall in Varied Environments — 80
   Overcoming Recall Challenges — 82

8. STEP SIX: LEASH WALKING — 85
   Introducing Your Puppy to Leash Walking — 88
   Addressing Pulling and Lunging on Leash — 90
   Safe Tie-Out Practices — 92

9. BUSY OWNERS 10-MINUTE TRAINING STRATEGIES — 95
   Blending Training into Everyday Activities — 98
   Maintaining Consistency Amidst a Busy Schedule — 99
   Tracking Progress and Celebrating Milestones — 101

10. POSITIVE REINFORCEMENT STRATEGIES — 104
    Choosing the Best Rewards for Your Puppy — 107
    Reinforcing Good Behavior in Real-Time — 109
    Adjusting Techniques for Different Temperaments — 111

11. MANAGING COMMON BEHAVIORAL ISSUES — 114
    Redirecting Destructive Chewing — 117
    Teaching Your Puppy Not to Bite — 119
    Tackling Jumping Up on People — 121
    Strategies for Calming Hyperactivity — 123

12. FOSTERING A LIFELONG BOND	126
Playtime for Mental and Physical Stimulation	129
Building Confidence Through New Experiences	130
Creating a Loving and Respectful Partnership	132
BONUS: 250 Puppy Names	135
Conclusion	137
References	143

Introduction

The day you have been waiting for has finally arrived! You're bringing a furry bundle of joy into your home—a new four-legged companion with eyes full of wonder, eager to explore every corner of the house. Watching your new companion dart around the living room, nose to the floor, you are struck by excitement and maybe are a little concerned. With life already brimming with work, family obligations, and never-ending tasks, how will you guide this eager pup into becoming the well-mannered, self-assured dream dog you envision?

No worries, the *Puppy Training Bible* is here to be your steadfast guide on this rewarding journey. Tailored for owners with packed schedules, this guide gives you 6 simple steps needed to give you a well-behaved dog without compromising your peace of mind or daily commitments. Packed with additional information, our Puppy Training Bible ensures you can nurture a content, well rounded dog at any age.

Throughout this book, I refer to your new addition as a companion or puppy, but rest assured, the training techniques outlined are equally effective for older pups and even adult or senior dogs. Regardless of age, these strategies can help transform your companion into the dog you've always wanted.

With over 20 years of experience, I've witnessed owners struggle to find adequate training methods that fit into their hectic lives. Through my experience with German Shepherds, I've developed a proven approach that combines positive reinforcement with a deep understanding of your puppy's instincts.

This book isn't about rigid rules or dominance-based techniques that leave you and your puppy stressed and confused. Instead, you'll discover how to turn training into a fun bonding experience that strengthens your relationship and brings out the best in your dog. By breaking down the process into six manageable steps, you'll gain the knowledge and confidence to navigate every stage of your puppy's development.

You'll learn how to:

- Prepare your home and gather essential supplies before your puppy's arrival
- Establish a consistent potty-training routine that sets your pup up for success
- Use crate training to create a safe space for your dog
- Prevent food aggression and teach polite mealtime manners
- Socialize your puppy to build confidence and adaptability
- Teach your dog to come when called, even in distracting environments
- Mastering Stress-Free Leash Walking and more

This book provides practical tips, examples, and easy-to-follow instructions that make training simple, even with your busy schedule. You'll gain a deeper understanding of your puppy's perspective, behavior, and body language, helping you to communicate well and build trust and respect.

With patience, consistency, and the guidance provided in these pages, you'll watch your puppy blossom into a well-mannered, confident companion who brings joy to your life for years to come.

Before getting started, let's consider naming your beautiful puppy. You'll find a list of over 250 names to inspire you at the back of this book. Begin by selecting your favorites, and when your puppy arrives, you'll quickly discover which name truly suits them.

Now, let's dive in and get ready to discover the power of positive, instinct-driven training. Your journey with the Puppy Training Bible, 6 Simple Steps starts now.

Chapter 1

Preparing for Your Puppy's Arrival

Bringing a new puppy home is an exciting experience. But with that excitement comes a whirlwind of responsibility that can be daunting. You may find yourself standing in a pet store aisle, surrounded by many products, unsure of what you truly need. It's easy to become overwhelmed, wondering if you've forgotten something crucial. This section is designed to cut through that confusion and set you on the path to success. By the time you finish reading, you'll know what you need before your puppy's paws cross the threshold of your home. The goal is to ensure those first days are seamless and stress-free, allowing you more time to focus on forming a bond with your new little companion.

Crafting Your Puppy Supply Checklist

Before diving into the responsibility that comes with a new puppy, having a well-thought-out checklist is important. This isn't just any list—it's your strategic plan for carefully navigating the initial days of puppy parenting. It's a comprehensive guide to ensuring you have everything at hand, streamlining those initial days of puppy parenthood.

Let's start with the basics: food and water bowls. These aren't just functional items; they set the stage for your puppy's daily routine. Opt for durable, non-skid bowls to prevent spills and messes, promoting a clean eating environment. Consider adjustable height bowls that accommodate growth, reduce neck strain, and encourage healthy posture during meals. When it comes to food, choose brands specifically formulated for puppies rich in nutrients to support their rapid growth and development. Consulting your vet can provide tailored recommendations based on your puppy's breed and size.

Comfort is key for your little one, so invest in bedding that offers warmth and support. Whether you choose a fluffy bed, a bolster bed, or simple blankets, ensure it's easy to clean and just the right size. This is where your puppy will retreat after a day of exploration, so make it inviting and safe. Chew toys are another must-have, essential for easing the teething process and providing mental stimulation. Select durable, safe, engaging toys that help redirect those sharp little teeth away from your furniture and shoes.

Health and safety are crucial for your puppy's well-being. Keep a first-aid kit tailored for puppies on hand to prepare you for minor accidents or injuries. Make sure it's stocked with antiseptic wipes, bandages, and tweezers. Flea and tick prevention products are a must from day one, safeguarding your puppy from pests that can cause discomfort or illness. Talk to your vet about the best options for your puppy's age and lifestyle.

Traveling with your puppy, whether it's the first trip home or future adventures, traveling requires thoughtful preparation. A secure travel crate or carrier is vital for safe transport. Look for one that is well-ventilated and sturdy, providing comfort and containment. Safety harnesses for car travel are non-negotiable, preventing injury and ensuring your puppy remains secure during the ride. Reflective harnesses can also enhance visibility during nighttime outings, offering an extra layer of safety.

Grooming supplies are often overlooked, yet they play an important role in maintaining your puppy's health and hygiene. Choose a puppy-safe shampoo and conditioner to keep their coat clean without irritation. Grooming your dog keeps your puppy looking and smelling great and strengthens your bond. Soft-bristle brushes are gentle on your puppy's sensitive skin, making grooming a pleasant experience rather than a chore. Begin grooming practices early, integrating them into your puppy's daily routine. Reward their cooperation with treats or praise to create positive experiences during grooming sessions.

Essential Checklist for Your New Puppy

- Feeding Supplies: Durable, non-skid food and water bowls; puppy-specific food.
- Comfort Items: Soft bedding; chew toys for teething.
- Health and Safety: Puppy first-aid kit, flea and tick prevention.
- Travel Essentials: Secure travel crate or carrier; safety harnesses.
- Grooming Tools: Puppy-safe shampoo, soft-bristle brushes.

This checklist ensures you are fully equipped for the whirlwind of introducing a puppy to your home. With each item, you'll reduce stress and feel confident knowing you are fully prepared for your new baby. This lets you focus on what truly matters—building a strong, lasting bond with your new best friend.

Puppy-Proofing Your Home for Safety

Welcoming a puppy into your home is similar to preparing for a lively toddler. Their boundless curiosity and energy mean everything within their reach becomes a potential hazard. As responsible owners, creating a safe environment is essential. Begin by conducting a thorough room-by-room inspection, imagining the world through your puppy's eyes. In the living room, check for electrical cords sprawling across the floor, representing a danger of burns or shocks. Consider concealing these cords using covers or securing them along the walls to prevent your inquisitive little puppy from chewing on them.

Creating designated safe zones in your home is a proactive measure to ensure your puppy's safety. Utilizing baby gates can prove essential because they limit access to areas where dangers are not easily alleviated. For example, with its abundance of hot surfaces and enticing aromas, the kitchen should be inaccessible in your absence. Setting up a puppy playpen provides a controlled area where your puppy can explore safely. This becomes their haven, filled with toys and comforts, offering them freedom without risk. It's a flexible solution, allowing you to manage your puppy's environment as they grow and become more adept at navigating their world.

Toxic plants and substances are another hidden danger many people don't consider. Common houseplants, like lilies, poinsettias, and philodendrons, can be harmful if ingested by your puppy. Removing or placing these plants out of reach is a simple yet effective way to prevent potential poisoning incidents. Educate yourself on which household items pose risks. Another consideration might be your cleaning supplies, which are often stored under sinks. These could be relocated to high cabinets or placed behind childproof latches. Even everyday items like sugarless gum containing xylitol can be highly toxic to dogs. By taking the time to identify and eliminate these hazards, you can create a safer, more welcoming home for your new companion.

Puppies, much like toddlers, are drawn to small, colorful objects. Coins, rubber bands, and small toys can quickly become choking hazards if left within reach. Relocating some of these items to elevated shelves or storage boxes will keep these items safely out of reach. This simple adjustment helps prevent accidents and ensures your puppy's environment is as safe as possible—additionally, secure trashcans with lids to deter your puppy from exploring inside. Exploring trashcans can lead puppies to discover bones, spoiled food, and other potentially dangerous items. Beyond the immediate risks, this behavior could also cultivate undesirable habits, potentially causing frustration for you and creating unnecessary challenges in your puppy's training and development.

Adapting your home for a puppy goes beyond eliminating dangers— creating an environment that nurtures their growth and wellbeing. It's a proactive approach to keep them safe, foster positive behaviors, and prevent potential bad habits from developing down the line. While this process requires time and effort, the peace of mind it brings is invaluable. Your puppy will explore, learn, and grow in a safe space, free to be their curious and playful self. By taking these steps, you can stop bad habits from developing.

Setting Up a Stress-Free Crate Space

Selecting the right crate is the first step in establishing a haven for your new companion. You might consider a crate that can adapt to your puppy's growth, such as those with adjustable dividers. A crate that feels too large can be intimidating, but more often than not, it encourages accidents, as it provides too much space to separate sleeping and potty areas. When your puppy is young, keep the space small and cozy, just enough for them to stand, turn around, and lie down comfortably. Many new puppy owners mistakenly believe that their pets need a lot of space to move around in their crates. However, this is not true. As I mentioned earlier, giving them a little extra room can lead them to use that space as a bathroom. Starting with a smaller, cozier area mimicking the snug, den-like environment dogs naturally seek is important. You can adjust the divider in their crate to gradually increase their living area as your puppy grows.

The placement of the crate in your home can significantly affect your puppy's acceptance of it. Choose a location that strikes a balance between being quiet and allowing for social engagement. A low-traffic area away from direct noise and commotion will help your puppy feel secure, yet positioning the crate near family activity areas ensures they don't feel isolated. For instance, placing the crate in a living room corner allows your puppy to observe and feel part of the family dynamic without being overwhelmed. This strategic placement helps your puppy associate the crate with safety and comfort rather than feeling like a punishment or exile. Avoiding areas with drafts or direct sunlight is important, as these can create discomfort and deter your puppy from using the crate willingly.

Additionally, you may want to contemplate your long-term plans for crate use. Once your pup is older, fully trained, and has demonstrated reliable behavior, you may wonder whether the crate should remain a permanent fixture. Considering this early allows for a smoother transition later, should you decide to retire the crate. Replacing it with a comfortable dog bed in the exact location offers a familiar yet new resting space for your trustworthy companion. The older pup may initially experience slight discomfort adjusting to this new change. Still, they will quickly adapt to their new bed, thanks to the familiarity of its placement.

The next step is to make the crate a cozy and inviting space. Introduce a few favorite toys or comfort items your puppy is already familiar with, helping them associate the crate with positive experiences. These items offer entertainment and a sense of familiarity, easing any anxiety your puppy might feel in this new setting. You may consider soft, washable bedding that provides warmth and comfort, transforming the crate into a personal retreat. This bedding should be easy to clean in case of accidents, ensuring a fresh environment for your puppy. Remember that puppies, in their youth, have a natural inclination to chew. They may chew on their beds and blankets out of boredom when left unattended. I recommend postponing the introduction of cushioned beds or blankets until they have matured and learned appropriate behaviors. However, this decision ultimately rests with you. Over time, the cozy space you've created and the positive associations with it will build trust and security, making the crate a beloved part of their daily routine.

Acclimating your puppy to the crate is a gradual process. Allowing your puppy to explore the crate on their terms is a good start. Leave the door open and place treats inside to encourage curiosity and exploration. This initial introduction shouldn't be rushed. Just let your puppy enter and exit freely without pressure. Gradually, as your puppy becomes more comfortable, close the door for short periods. Remain nearby so your puppy can see you. Use a calm, reassuring voice to praise and reward your puppy with treats for staying inside the crate quietly. This reward-based approach reinforces the idea that the crate is a positive place, associated with good things like treats and affection.

Patience is key during this phase. If your puppy shows signs of distress, such as whining or scratching, resist the urge to let them out immediately, as this can inadvertently teach them that fussing leads to freedom. Instead, wait for a moment of calm and quiet before opening the door, rewarding them for their patience. Gradually increase your puppy's time in the crate, ensuring each experience is positive and reassuring. Through consistent practice and positive reinforcement, your puppy will see the crate as a safe, comforting space to relax and feel secure.

Scheduling Your First Vet Visit

One of the most critical steps in laying a strong foundation for your puppy's health is scheduling that first vet visit. This initial meeting is not just a routine check-up; it's a vital opportunity to establish your puppy's health baseline. A thorough examination will help identify potential issues early, ensuring your puppy starts life with a clean bill of health. During this visit, the veterinarian will assess your puppy's overall physical condition, check for common ailments, and initiate an appropriate vaccination schedule. Vaccinations are crucial as they protect your puppy from diseases such as parvovirus and distemper. By getting these shots on time, you safeguard your puppy's health and contribute to preventing these diseases from spreading in the canine community.

Finding a vet that aligns with your values and expectations is essential. Consider the clinic's location and hours; a vet close to home with flexible hours can make appointments more convenient, especially in emergencies. Look for a vet with experience in puppy care, as they'll be more attuned to the needs of caring for young dogs. You might also want to ask other pet owners in your community for recommendations, ensuring your chosen vet has a good reputation for expertise and compassion.

Preparing for the first vet visit can feel overwhelming, but a bit of organization goes a long way. Bring any health records you received from the breeder or shelter, as these provide valuable insights into your puppy's past care and vaccination status. Make a list of any behaviors or concerns you've observed, no matter how minor they seem. This can include unusual eating habits, excessive scratching, or anything else that doesn't seem typical. This information helps the vet make a comprehensive assessment and address any potential issues before they escalate.

During the visit, take the opportunity to discuss long-term care plans with the vet. Setting up future appointments and creating a vaccination timetable ensures that your puppy receives consistent care. It's also a good time to talk about spaying or neutering, which has health and behavioral benefits for your dog. Your vet can provide guidance on the best age for this procedure based on your puppy's breed and health status. Discussing a plan for regular check-ups will help keep your puppy healthy and thriving as they grow.

In these first few weeks, you're not just welcoming a pet into your home but embarking on a new chapter of companionship. Each action you take—puppy-proofing your home or arranging that initial vet visit—lays the groundwork for a lifetime of shared experiences. Your puppy relies on you for love, care, and guidance, and in return, you'll gain a friend who will enrich your life in many ways. With the right preparation and dedication, you're on your way to nurturing a well-adjusted, healthy dog who will be by your side through everything.

Chapter 2

Bringing Your Puppy Home

Today marks the beginning of a new journey as you open your heart and home to welcome your new puppy. This is a pivotal moment, the beginning of a lifelong bond, yet the transition can be overwhelming for your puppy, who has just left the comfort of a familiar environment. A gradual introduction to their new home is essential to ease this transition. Slowly acquainting your puppy with their surroundings helps prevent sensory overload and fosters a sense of security.

Start by allowing your puppy to explore one room at a time. This controlled exploration is crucial in preventing them from feeling overwhelmed by the vastness of an unfamiliar space. Supervise their interactions with household items, guiding them gently away from potential hazards. Remember, your home is a treasure trove of new sights, sounds, and smells. Your puppy's natural curiosity will lead them to investigate everything. Keeping a watchful eye ensures their safety and helps you redirect their attention to safe, appropriate activities when necessary. As your puppy becomes familiar with each room, gradually expand their access, allowing them to grow more comfortable and confident in their new environment.

The atmosphere in your home during those first few days can significantly impact your puppy's adjustment. Aim for a calm and quiet arrival to ease the transition. Limit the number of people present to prevent overwhelming your new puppy with too many faces and voices. While friends and family may be eager to meet the newest member of the household, it's wise to stagger introductions over several days. Keeping noise levels low initially helps create a serene environment, allowing your puppy to acclimate without added stress. This peaceful setting not only aids in their adjustment but also sets the tone for a harmonious relationship built on trust and understanding.

Scent plays an intriguing role in familiarizing your puppy with their new surroundings. Consider placing a blanket or toy from the breeder or shelter in your home. These familiar scents provide comfort and reassurance, acting as a bridge between the past and the present. Additionally, introduce your puppy to the scents of family members by allowing them to sniff clothing or hands gently. This sense of smell helps your puppy feel more comfortable, reducing anxiety and fostering a sense of belonging. As they become accustomed to these scents, your puppy will associate them with safety and companionship, reinforcing their growing trust in you and your family.

Consistency is paramount in helping your puppy acclimate. Keep furniture and items in predictable locations, allowing your puppy to navigate their surroundings confidently. Routine is comforting, and your puppy will thrive in an environment where they know what to expect. This predictability extends to daily activities, such as feeding times and walks, helping to instill a sense of security and routine. Maintaining this stability provides your puppy with a foundation of familiarity and comfort, which is essential for their emotional and psychological well-being.

Reflection Section: Welcoming Your Puppy

Take a moment to reflect on your current home environment. Consider the following questions: Which room will you introduce your puppy to first? How can you create a calm atmosphere for your puppy's arrival? What familiar scents can you incorporate to comfort your puppy? By contemplating these aspects, you prepare to offer a seamless and nurturing introduction to your home, ensuring your puppy feels welcome and secure.

As you begin this next section, remember that patience and consistency are your allies. Your puppy is learning not just about its new home but also about you and the world around it. By taking these thoughtful steps, you lay the groundwork for a trusting, loving relationship that will flourish over time.

Creating a First-Day Routine for Success

The first day with your new puppy sets the stage for what lies ahead. Establishing a structured routine from the beginning is not just about order; it's about creating a predictable environment where your puppy feels secure and settled. Start with a detailed timetable that includes scheduled feeding times and regular bathroom breaks. Knowing when to expect meals can help alleviate your puppy's anxiety in a new home. Feed your puppy at the same time each day, and take them outside immediately after to establish a consistent potty routine. This helps with house training and helps your puppy understand that certain activities follow others, reinforcing a sense of stability.

Balancing play and rest periods are crucial in maintaining your puppy's well-being. While their energy seems boundless, puppies can quickly become overstimulated, leading to crankiness or destructive behavior. Incorporate short play sessions into your schedule, allowing your puppy to burn off energy without becoming overwhelmed. These sessions can be as simple as a game of fetch or exploring a new toy. Equally important is designating quiet time for naps and rest. Providing a calm, cozy, relaxing space will ensure they recharge and remain in good spirits. This balance between activity and downtime helps regulate your puppy's energy levels and increases their happiness.

From day one, setting clear boundaries to prevent confusion and establish household rules is essential. Designating no-go areas in your home can protect your belongings and your puppy. Gates or closed doors can keep curious noses out of rooms that might be hazardous or off-limits. Alongside physical boundaries, begin introducing acceptable behavior patterns. Reinforce these through gentle correction and praise, helping your puppy learn what is expected of them. For instance, discourage jumping up on your leg for attention or jumping on furniture if that's not allowed, or teach them to sit before new visitors. Consistency is key here; by maintaining the same rules from the start, you prevent mixed messages later that can confuse your puppy and lead to unwanted bad habits.

Training shouldn't be seen as a separate task but something you integrate into your daily activities. Meal times offer a perfect opportunity to introduce basic commands like "sit" or "stay." Before placing the food bowl down, ask your puppy to sit, rewarding them with their meal once they comply. This not only teaches obedience but also patience. Throughout the day, practice name recognition by calling your puppy during interactions. Use a cheerful tone, and reward them when they respond. These brief training sessions, spread throughout the day, help reinforce your puppy's learning without overwhelming them. They also help build a foundation of communication between you and your pet, making future training more manageable.

Remember, your puppy is absorbing everything during these early days. Establishing a routine that includes structured activities, clear boundaries, and integrated training creates a nurturing environment where your puppy feels safe and loved. This approach aids their adjustment and fosters a strong, trusting relationship. As you engage in these routines, you'll find that your puppy isn't just learning from you; you're learning from them, too. Every interaction is an opportunity to understand each other's rhythms, needs, and quirks, laying the groundwork for a harmonious coexistence.

Building Initial Trust and Bonding

Establishing trust with your puppy from the very start is fundamental. Positive reinforcement is a powerful tool in this process, offering a simple yet effective way to communicate that your puppy is safe and loved. Whenever your puppy exhibits calm behavior, take the opportunity to reward them. A small treat can be a delightful surprise, reinforcing that being quiet and composed brings good things. Alongside treats, verbal affirmations work wonders. A soft, encouraging voice saying, "Good dog," can convey warmth and approval, helping your puppy feel secure. The repeated assurance that you're a source of comfort, not fear, which builds the foundation of trust.

Physical touch is another vital aspect of bonding with your puppy. Gentle handling communicates care and respect, something your puppy will respond to instinctively. When petting, use a soft touch, especially around sensitive areas like the ears and belly. This gentle approach not only calms your puppy but also deepens your connection. Grooming sessions can also be bonding moments. They allow you to interact closely; your puppy learns to associate these sessions with positive feelings. When holding or carrying your puppy, support their body fully, providing comfort and stability. This reassures them they are safe in your arms, fostering trust and security.

Playtime is not just about burning off energy; it's an opportunity to strengthen your bond with your puppy. Interactive play, where both you and your puppy are engaged, enhances your relationship. Games like fetch or tug-of-war are not only fun but also teach your puppy to follow rules and boundaries in a joyful setting. Toys that require your participation make play more interactive. These sessions are more than just fun; they're moments of shared joy that build mutual understanding and trust. Through play, your puppy learns you're not just a provider of food and shelter but a companion in fun and adventure.

Consistency in your interactions with your puppy is crucial for reinforcing the bond. Regular one-on-one time with your puppy helps them understand they are a valued part of your life. It's not about the duration but the quality of time spent together. Whether it's a short walk, a few quiet moments of petting, or simply sitting together in a peaceful spot, these moments of connection are invaluable. Introducing family members gradually allows your puppy to build familiarity and comfort with each person. Over time, these consistent, positive interactions help your puppy establish a sense of belonging within your family.

Such interactions lay the groundwork for a stronger bond with each passing day. By integrating positive reinforcement, gentle touch, playful engagement, and consistent interaction, you create an environment where trust can flourish. Your puppy learns to look to you for guidance, comfort, and companionship, knowing they are loved and protected.

Minimizing Separation Anxiety from Day One

Separation anxiety is a common challenge for many new puppy owners. It can manifest in behaviors such as whining, barking, or even destructive chewing when your puppy is left alone. Addressing this early ensures your puppy grows into a confident and independent dog. Start by introducing short periods of absence. This doesn't mean leaving your puppy alone for hours right away; instead, begin with brief separations. Step into another room for just a few minutes, then return calmly. Gradually increase the duration of these absences as your puppy becomes more comfortable. This slow introduction helps your puppy understand that while you may leave, you always come back. It builds their confidence in being alone without fear or anxiety.

Comfort items can significantly help reduce your puppy's separation anxiety. A soft toy or blanket with your scent can provide immense solace in your absence. Before leaving, gently rub a toy or blanket on your skin, transferring your scent. This familiar smell is reassuring, reminding your puppy of your care and affection. These items become a source of comfort and help your puppy feel connected to you, even when you're not physically present. Additionally, consider rotating these comfort items to maintain their novelty and effectiveness.

Another effective strategy is creating a comforting environment. A soothing atmosphere can make a difference for a puppy learning to cope with being alone. Playing soft music or leaving a ticking clock nearby can mimic the comforting sounds of a heartbeat, which is especially comforting for young puppies. These background noises can help drown out startling sounds from outside and provide a soothing backdrop to their alone time. The goal is to create an environment where your puppy feels safe and relaxed, reducing the likelihood of anxiety-driven behaviors.

Establishing a calm departure and arrival routine can significantly reduce the anxiety your puppy experiences. Avoid dramatic goodbyes that might heighten your puppy's awareness of your absence. Instead, keep departures low-key and routine. A simple pat and a soft "see you later" can suffice. When you return, resist the urge to make a big fuss. Instead, greet your puppy calmly and reward them for staying composed. This reinforces the idea that your comings and goings are normal and not events to be anxious about. Over time, your puppy will learn to anticipate your return without distress.

Incorporating these strategies lays the groundwork for an independent and well-adjusted puppy. You teach them that being alone is not something to fear but a regular part of their day. This reduces stress for you and your puppy, paving the way for a harmonious living environment. As you nurture this independence, you'll find that your puppy becomes more resilient and adaptable, ready to handle new experiences with confidence. This foundation is essential for your puppy's training and development, ensuring they grow into a balanced, happy companion.

Bonus Section: Naming Your New Puppy

As a special bonus, I've included a comprehensive list of popular dog names at the end of this book. This list of names might be the perfect match for your puppy's unique personality. If not directly, it could ignite your creativity, leading you to discover the ideal name.

Choosing the right name for your puppy is crucial, as it's one of the first steps in establishing a strong bond. A name helps your puppy recognize they are being addressed and begins their journey of adapting and learning. If you're still searching for that perfect name, now's the time to decide.

Observing your puppy's emerging personality can offer inspiration.

Selecting your puppy's name is a memorable occasion, but finding one that perfectly reflects their unique character might take some time. Here are some tips to guide you.

Pick short and sweet names with one or two syllables. These are easier for your puppy to recognize and simpler for you to call out during training.

End with a vowel: Dogs are more responsive to names ending in a vowel, as they can differentiate frequency ranges better than humans.

Avoid Negative or Offensive Names: Choose a respectful and positive name to ensure a healthy relationship with your puppy.

Distinguish from Other Pets: If you have multiple pets, select a name distinct from the others to avoid confusion.

Steer Clear of Command-like Names: Names that resemble commands, such as "Sit" or "Stay," could lead to unnecessary confusion during training sessions. (Such as Kit or Kay)

Conduct the Nickname Test: Consider potential nicknames to ensure they are appropriate and not similar to other pets' names or commands.

Reflect on Your Puppy's Personality: The name should resonate with your puppy's individuality and character.

Consistency is Key: Once chosen, stick with the name. Consistency helps in faster learning and adaptation. If a name change is necessary, choose a new name that sounds similar to the old one.

Finding Inspiration for Puppy Names: Inspiration can come from various sources, such as literature, movies, or history. The key is to choose a name you're comfortable calling out in any setting, ensuring it's one you'd proudly use at the dog park or in front of family.

Teaching Your Puppy Their Name

After selecting a name, the next step is ensuring your puppy recognizes and responds to it. This process is fundamental for all future training and commands.

Your puppy's name should be a cue for their attention, signaling you're addressing them directly. It should not be used for scolding or as a recall command, which could lead to negative associations or confusion. Use their name to capture attention before giving a command and in positive, encouraging contexts. Don't use their name for punishment, not as a recall command, or in negative situations.

Mark & Reward - When your puppy looks at you upon hearing their name, immediately reward them with a treat and praise.

Capture Their Attention - In a distraction-free environment, call their name cheerfully. If they don't respond, try again with a gentle clap to capture their attention.

Lose and Regain Attention - Allow your puppy to become briefly distracted before calling their name again, rewarding their response each time.

Repetition is Key - Repeat the process in short, engaging sessions to keep their attention and reinforce the association between their name and your attention.

Practice in Various Settings - Gradually introduce new environments for training, from quiet indoor spaces to more distracting outdoor areas.

Public Training - Practice calling your puppy's name in public spaces, starting with less distracting environments and gradually increasing the level of distraction.

Introduce Distractions - As your puppy improves, add distractions to the training, rewarding them for choosing to focus on you.

Increase Attention Span - Over time, extend the duration your puppy maintains attention before rewarding them.

Ongoing Training - Even after your puppy has learned their name, continuous practice in varied settings is crucial. Training should always be a positive experience, ending on a high note to encourage eagerness for future sessions. Through consistency and patience, your puppy will learn to respond to their name reliably, laying the foundation for a lifetime of communication and bonding.

Chapter 3

Step One: Potty Training

It's a new day and a fresh opportunity to continue guiding your furry friend toward becoming a well-mannered member of your household. Potty training is at the heart of this journey, a crucial step in teaching your puppy where and when to relieve themselves. While it may seem daunting, establishing a solid potty training routine can transform this challenge into an achievable goal. With a consistent schedule, you prevent accidents and help your puppy understand the rhythm of your shared daily life.

Creating a regular schedule forms the backbone of successful potty training. Puppies, much like human toddlers, thrive on predictability. By designating specific times for bathroom breaks, you teach your puppy when to expect these moments of relief. Always take your puppy out immediately after meals or naps. This consistency reinforces the connection between specific activities and bathroom breaks, making it clear to your puppy when it's time to go. Early morning and late evening routines are essential, as these times will frame the puppy's day and night. A morning trip outside right after waking sets a positive tone for the day, while a final potty break before bedtime helps them settle for the night.

Adapting a potty schedule to fit your daily routine while meeting your puppy's needs requires some thought. Puppies have their natural rhythms, often needing to relieve themselves after eating, drinking, sleeping, or playing. Incorporate these natural patterns into your schedule to create a balance between your needs and theirs.

Verbal and non-verbal cues are powerful tools in potty training, facilitating communication between you and your puppy. Simple phrases like "go potty" or "potty time" signal what you expect from your puppy when you take them outside. Consistently using these words helps your puppy associate them with going potty. Hand signals or gestures can complement verbal cues, particularly in noisy environments, or as a backup if your puppy is distracted. These cues create a clear line of communication, reducing confusion and reinforcing the desired behavior.

Life is full of unpredictability, and maintaining a rigid schedule isn't always feasible. Flexibility is key to navigating unexpected changes without derailing your puppy's progress. Prepare for situations like travel or unusual work hours by planning alternative arrangements. A trusted friend or neighbor might step in to assist, or you may adjust the timing of meals to align with a temporary schedule. Weather changes, illness, or other disruptions may require a brief adjustment in routine. The goal is not to be perfect but to remain consistent enough that your puppy feels secure in their potty training.

Journaling for Success: A journal can be an invaluable tool in this process, allowing you to track your puppy's training habits and adjust accordingly. Record when they eat, drink, and go potty. Over time, patterns will emerge, helping you refine the schedule to suit both of you. This journal will be invaluable as behaviors change and you begin training in other areas. It will also help communicate to other family members how the training has been going and what is working and what is not. This communication and personalization ensures your puppy's needs are met without disrupting your day-to-day life.

Reflection Section: Tailoring Your Potty Schedule

Consider your current routine and how it aligns with your puppy's needs. Reflect on the following: What adjustments can you make to integrate your puppy's natural rhythms? How can you incorporate verbal and non-verbal cues into your routine? This proactive approach ensures you provide the structure your puppy needs while maintaining the flexibility required by life's unexpected turns. This balance cultivates a positive potty training experience for you and your new companion.

Recognizing Your Puppy's Potty Cues

As you spend time with your new puppy, you'll notice they have their own way of communicating their needs, especially regarding potty time. Recognizing these cues is key to successful potty training. Imagine your puppy sniffing around the floor, nose diligently following an invisible trail. This behavior often signals their search for the perfect potty spot. Another classic sign is when they start to circle or pace restlessly, almost as if caught in an internal debate. These actions are not random; they're your puppy's way of telling you they're ready to go.

Observing your puppy's behavior closely allows you to become attuned to their unique signals, which can differ from one pup to another. Changes in their daily routine or diet might shift how they express their need to go outside. Perhaps your puppy starts pacing more frequently after switching to a new food or exhibits increased sniffing behavior when guests are visiting. By paying attention to these subtle signs, you gain insight into your puppy's comfort and readiness, allowing you to anticipate their bathroom needs before they become urgent. This awareness creates a smoother potty training experience for both of you.

Once you've identified your puppy's potty cues, reinforcing positive behavior becomes essential. Immediately rewarding your puppy after they do their business outside strengthens the connection between the action and the desired outcome. Use treats as a form of immediate praise, ensuring the reward is given right after they finish. This timing is crucial, as it helps your puppy associate their behavior with the reward. Adding a clicker to your training arsenal can further enhance this process. The distinct sound of the clicker, followed by a treat, serves as a clear marker of correct behavior, helping your puppy make the connection quickly and effectively.

As your puppy matures, their cues will evolve, and so should your approach. During growth spurts or development phases, your puppy's behavior may change, requiring you to adapt your training methods. If you notice your puppy sniffing around more after meals, this might indicate a new cue that needs attention. By staying observant and flexible, you ensure your potty training methods remain effective as your puppy grows.

Troubleshooting Common Potty Training Issues

Navigating the ups and downs of potty training can be like riding a roller coaster. When you think you've figured it all out, an unexpected accident can make you question everything. Whether it's the puppies' fault or your busy schedule, these mishaps are part of the process and will offer valuable learning opportunities. When an accident occurs, it's important to manage it constructively. The first step is to clean the area thoroughly with an enzyme-based cleaner. These products are specially formulated to break down the proteins in pet urine, effectively removing the scent that might otherwise encourage your puppy to return to the crime scene. Avoid reacting negatively or punishing your puppy; you don't want to create anxiety because this can lead to more accidents. Instead, reinforce positive behavior by praising your puppy when they go in the right spot, clarifying what actions earn them approval.

Regression can be disheartening, especially when you thought you were making progress. It's not uncommon for puppies to slip back into old habits, especially during transition or stress. When this happens, revisiting the basics can help reestablish what was learned. Return to more frequent potty breaks and reinforce foundational training techniques to remind your puppy of the correct behavior. If the regression persists, and you're concerned about your puppy's health, consulting a veterinarian can provide clarity. Underlying health conditions such as urinary tract infections could compromise your puppy's bladder control. Consulting a veterinarian can help diagnose and address these issues effectively.

External factors can have a surprising impact on your puppy's potty behavior. Changing household dynamics, such as a new family member or pet, can disrupt your puppy's routine and cause setbacks. Similarly, environmental shifts, like moving to a new home or changes in the weather, can alter your puppy's comfort level when going outside. Rain or snow might make outdoor potty trips less appealing, leading to reluctance or hesitation. Being mindful of these factors can help you adapt your training approach. Using a covered area for potty breaks during inclement weather or gradually introducing your puppy to new environments with patience and encouragement can help them adjust.

Stubbornness: Some puppies are more stubborn than others, requiring more creativity and persistence to overcome potty training challenges. For particularly stubborn cases, enrolling in a training class or seeking professional advice from a dog trainer can provide additional support. Trainers bring experience and insight that might uncover the missing piece in your training puzzle.

Potty Bells: Tools like potty bells can be effective in teaching your puppy to signal when it needs to go outside.

Hang a bell by the door and encourage your puppy to nudge it before a potty break. With consistency and repetition, your puppy will learn to associate ringing the bell with the need to go out, giving it a clear method of communication. This is helpful for busy puppy parents as well!

Using Potty Pads and Outdoor Training Techniques

In the landscape of potty training, potty pads have emerged as a convenient option, particularly those that are living in apartments or homes with limited outdoor access. These absorbent pads offer a safe space for your puppy to relieve themselves indoors, reducing the risk of accidents on carpets or hardwood floors. Potty pads can be a lifesaver for city dwellers or during harsh weather conditions, providing an indoor solution when outdoor excursions aren't feasible. However, while they offer convenience, it's essential to recognize their potential drawbacks. Over-reliance on potty pads can delay or complicate the transition to outdoor potty training, as puppies might get used to the comfort of indoor relief. If you must use puppy pads, try to prevent this over-reliance by gradually introducing your puppy to outdoor potty habits as they become accustomed to using pads. Start by placing the pad near the door and slowly move it outside, encouraging your puppy to follow. This step-by-step transition helps your puppy understand that the ultimate goal is to go outside.

Establishing successful outdoor potty habits begins with choosing a consistent location in your yard or nearby park. This designated area becomes familiar to your puppy, where they can relax and focus on the task. Consistency is key—using the same location helps your puppy associate the spot with going potty, reducing distractions and confusion. Keep your puppy on a leash to guide and control them when venturing outside. The leash gently reminds them of your presence and guidance, encouraging them to stay on task. This approach is helpful in environments bustling with new sights and sounds, where your puppy might be tempted to wander. By guiding them to one specific area, you help them understand the purpose of the outing, reinforcing the habit through repetition and familiarity.

For many owners, a flexible approach combining potty pads and outdoor training can offer the best of both worlds. This hybrid method allows you to adapt to changing weather conditions or personal convenience without disrupting your puppy's training progress. On days when the weather is uncooperative, having the option to use a potty pad indoors ensures your puppy has a consistent place to go. When the sun shines and the outdoors beckons, you can switch to outdoor training, maintaining the continuity of your cues and rewards. This method requires a bit of extra effort to maintain consistency. Still, providing your puppy with a well-rounded understanding of acceptable potty locations pays off. Whether indoors or out, ensure your puppy receives the same verbal cues and rewards for successful behavior, reinforcing their learning across environments.

Patience and persistence are the cornerstones of successful potty training, regardless of the techniques used. Every puppy progresses at their own pace, and it's important to celebrate small victories along the way. Each time your puppy understands a new cue or successfully transitions from pad to outdoor space, take a moment to acknowledge the progress. These small victories build a foundation of confidence for both you and your puppy, encouraging continued learning and adaptation. Remember, setbacks are a natural part of the process. Your puppy is learning a complex skill that takes time to grasp fully. Approach each new day patiently, understanding that consistency and encouragement will eventually lead to long-term success.

As you navigate the world of potty training, remember that the journey is unique to you and your puppy. The techniques you choose should align with your lifestyle and your puppy's needs, creating an environment where both of you can thrive. With patience, persistence, and some flexibility, you'll guide your puppy toward becoming a well-trained member of your household. This section concludes with the understanding that all these efforts lead to a harmonious coexistence, paving the way for a lifetime of companionship. As you move forward, keep in mind that each step you take together strengthens your relationship and prepares you for the next exciting challenges.

Chapter 4

Step Two: Crate Training

This is where the art of selecting the right crate comes into play, providing your puppy with an ideal balance of safety and comfort. Choosing the perfect crate size is pivotal, as it significantly influences your puppy's willingness to embrace their new space. A crate that's too small can lead to discomfort and restlessness, while one too large may not provide the snug, den-like feel that puppies instinctively seek. To find the right fit, measure your puppy's length from nose to tail and height from floor to head, adding a few inches for comfort. This ensures they have ample room to stand, turn, and lie down comfortably, fostering a sense of security as they grow.

The world of dog crates is as varied as the puppies that inhabit them, offering a range of materials and designs to suit different needs. Wire crates, for instance, are a popular choice due to their excellent visibility and ventilation. They create an open environment where your puppy can observe their surroundings while still feeling enclosed. However, for puppies that thrive in more secluded spaces, a plastic crate might be more appropriate. These crates offer a den-like atmosphere, providing the privacy and security that some dogs prefer. They're also great for travel, with sturdy constructions that make them ideal for car trips.

On the other hand, soft-sided crates offer portability and are perfect for lighter travel needs or temporary setups. They provide a comfortable, flexible enclosure that can be easily folded away. However, these items may not be suitable for puppies who chew or dig.

Safety is a non-negotiable factor in choosing the right crate, as it ensures your puppy's well-being during their time inside. Look for crates with secure latches that prevent accidental escapes, keeping your puppy safely contained. Rounded edges are also important, minimizing the risk of injury from sharp corners. These features protect your puppy and provide peace of mind, knowing that their environment is as safe as it is comfortable. As you explore crate options, consider your puppy's specific needs and behaviors, ensuring the crate you choose aligns with their unique personality and tendencies.

Adaptability and versatility are key when choosing a crate that will grow with your puppy. Look for crates with adjustable dividers, allowing you to modify the space as your puppy grows. This feature is handy for young puppies, providing them with a snug space that can be expanded as they grow bigger. Collapsible designs are another valuable asset, offering easy storage and transport when needed. These practical features ensure that your investment in a crate provides long-term value, accommodating your puppy's changing needs while maintaining a consistent and familiar environment. As you begin this journey of crate training, remember that each choice you make plays a crucial role in shaping your puppy's experience, helping them find comfort and security in their own little corner of the world.

Introducing Your Puppy to the Crate

Among the many tasks at hand, introducing your puppy to their crate is fundamental to creating a safe and comforting environment. Start by allowing your puppy to explore the crate freely. Place it in a common area where your puppy often roams, and let them investigate at their own pace. Curiosity is natural; this initial exploration helps your puppy become familiar with the crate's presence without feeling pressured. Keep the door open during this stage to avoid any sense of confinement, allowing your puppy to understand that the crate is a choice, not a punishment.

A crucial part of this introduction is using treats to encourage your puppy to enter and explore the crate. Place a few small treats just inside the entrance, enticing them to step in and investigate. As they gain confidence, gradually place treats further inside, encouraging them to venture deeper. This method creates a positive association with the crate, transforming it into a place of reward and comfort. Each time your puppy enters, offer gentle praise and a treat, reinforcing that the crate is a safe, welcoming space. Approach this journey with patience, it helps your puppy develop trust and acclimate to the crate in their own time. Over time, this consistent encouragement builds a strong, positive connection between your puppy and their crate. The goal is to make the crate a place where your puppy feels secure and relaxed, associating it with good things rather than fear or confinement.

Familiar items can significantly ease your puppy's transition into crate life. Consider placing a favorite blanket or toy inside the crate—something that smells like mom or home. These items provide comfort and familiarity, acting as a bridge between the new environment and the scents they associate with safety and love. A cherished blanket's soft texture and familiar smell can be soothing, helping your puppy feel more at ease inside their crate. This simple addition can transform the crate from a mere structure into a comforting haven, fostering a sense of belonging and security.

The crate's location within your home can significantly impact your puppy's comfort. Ideally, place the crate near social areas where your family spends time, offering company without overstimulation. This positioning allows your puppy to observe daily activities and feel included, reducing feelings of isolation. However, ensure the crate is not in direct sunlight or drafty areas, as these can cause discomfort and deter your puppy from using the crate willingly. The right balance between social interaction and a peaceful retreat is key to successful crate placement.

Following these steps, you create a nurturing environment that encourages your puppy to view their crate as a safe, positive space. This foundation is crucial for building trust and ensuring your puppy feels secure in their new home. As your puppy becomes more accustomed to the crate, it becomes an integral part of their routine, providing a sanctuary for rest, relaxation, and reflection. Through patience, consistency, and positive reinforcement, the crate becomes more than just a training tool—it becomes a cherished part of your puppy's life, offering comfort and security as they grow and explore the world around them.

Making the Crate a Positive Space

Creating a positive association between your puppy and their crate is key to successful crate training. It starts with using the crate as a designated space for relaxation and downtime. By scheduling regular nap times in the crate, you establish a routine that signals to your puppy that the crate is a place for rest. This consistency helps your puppy understand that the crate is their retreat, a haven where they can unwind without interruptions. Over time, your puppy will associate the crate with these peaceful moments, making it a cherished part of their day.

Integrating the crate into your puppy's daily routine is another effective way to reinforce positive associations. Feeding your puppy in their crate is a practical strategy that combines nourishment with comfort. By placing their food bowl inside the crate, you encourage your puppy to enter willingly, associating the crate with the pleasant mealtime experience. This simple act reinforces that the crate is a safe and rewarding place. In addition to feeding, encourage quiet play with chew toys inside the crate. Offering a favorite toy or a tasty chew can keep your puppy engaged, transforming the crate into an enjoyable space rather than a confining one. These activities make the crate a regular part of your puppy's routine and build a sense of security and contentment within its walls.

Avoiding negative associations with the crate is crucial to fostering a positive relationship between your puppy and their new space. Never use the crate as a form of punishment. This can lead to fear and anxiety, undermining your efforts to create a safe and welcoming environment. Similarly, avoid forcing your puppy into the crate or abruptly closing the door. These actions can cause distress and hesitation, making your puppy reluctant to enter the crate willingly. Instead, focus on creating a positive, inviting atmosphere where your puppy feels comfortable and safe. By steering clear of negative experiences, you help your puppy view the crate as a positive space, encouraging voluntary use and reducing resistance.

Patience and gradual adjustment are the cornerstones of successful crate training. Allow your puppy to set the pace for their comfort, giving them the time to acclimate to the crate without pressure. Each puppy is unique; some may need more time than others to feel at ease. Gradually increase your puppy's time in the crate as they grow more comfortable, providing reassurance and positive reinforcement. This approach ensures your puppy associates the crate with positive experiences, building trust and security. As your puppy becomes more accustomed to the crate, you'll find that it naturally becomes a part of their routine. This gentle, patient crate training method helps your puppy adjust. It strengthens your bond, reinforcing your role as a source of safety and care.

Gradual Crate Training for Success

Crate training is not a sprint but a marathon, requiring a thoughtful and phased approach to ensure your puppy's comfort and acceptance. Begin by familiarizing your puppy with short periods in the crate while you remain nearby. This reassures them that the crate is a secure place, not a lonely exile. Sit quietly in the same room, allowing your puppy to observe your presence and feel reassured. As days progress, slowly extend your puppy's time in the crate and start stepping out of the room for brief periods. This gradual increase helps the puppy adjust to being alone without feeling abandoned. Each time you return, remain calm and composed, avoiding any fuss that might inadvertently reinforce anxiety about your departures.

Separation anxiety is a common concern during crate training, but effective strategies exist to mitigate it. Practice leaving the room while your puppy is crated, starting with a minute or two and gradually increasing the duration. Your calm return teaches your puppy that your absence is temporary and there is nothing to fear. Reinforcing calm behavior upon your return with gentle praise or a small treat helps your puppy associate you coming and going with a positive experience, reducing anxiety over time. Consistency is key, and by following a routine, your puppy learns to anticipate and adapt to your schedule, which builds their confidence and independence.

Incorporating the crate into your puppy's nighttime routine requires a delicate balance of comfort and consistency. Initially, you could place the crate in your bedroom close enough for your puppy to sense your presence. This proximity offers reassurance and helps ease any nighttime jitters. If your puppy seems restless or anxious, consider using a cover to create a den-like atmosphere. The cover provides a sense of enclosure, reducing visual stimuli and promoting a feeling of security. This setup not only aids in settling your puppy for the night but also establishes the crate as a safe haven for rest. Over time, you may gradually move the crate to a preferred location, reinforcing the crate's role as a consistent part of your puppy's daily life.

Successful crate training is built on the foundation of consistency. By setting a schedule for crating times and adhering to it, you communicate to your puppy that the crate is a reliable element of their daily life. This routine establishes a sense of security and predictability for your puppy. Everyone in the household must follow the same training protocol, ensuring the crate's role is consistently communicated. Variations in training can confuse your puppy and erode the trust and comfort you've worked to establish. With a united front, you solidify the crate's position as a positive, secure space in your puppy's perception. Establishing regular crating times and sticking to them helps your puppy understand a crate is a stable part of their routine. This regularity strengthens their sense of security and predictability. Any deviation can confuse your puppy, undermining the trust and comfort you've worked hard to build.

As you progress with crate training, patience and observation are your allies. Watch for cues from your puppy that indicate how they're adapting, and be ready to adjust your approach as needed. Some may quickly embrace the crate, while others take more time to feel at ease. Maintaining a unified approach reinforces the crate's status as a positive, safe space in your puppy's world.

In the next section, we'll explore the dynamics of preventing food aggression, an important step in ensuring peaceful, safe mealtimes for you and your puppy.

Chapter 5

Step Three: Preventing Food Aggression

In the wild, dogs' ancestors faced fierce competition for resources. This led to behaviors like guarding food to ensure survival. Even in a home filled with love and plenty, puppies can still exhibit these instincts, seeing their meals as precious treasures to protect. To understand and address it, we must first explore the instincts shaping your puppy's food approach.

In a litter, puppies often compete for food, racing to get their share before it's gone. This competitive feeding environment can translate into fast eating habits when they join a new household. While it's normal for your puppy to eat quickly, aggressive growling or snapping when approached during meals could signal a deeper issue. Occasional defensive postures are typical, like a stiffened body or a hard stare when disturbed. Still, if they escalate, they warrant closer attention. Recognizing the difference between normal and concerning behaviors is crucial in preventing food aggression from becoming a persistent problem.

Observing your puppy's feeding patterns provides insight into their behavior. Regular meal times and a consistent pace can indicate comfort and confidence. At the same time, irregular eating or signs of distress might suggest underlying issues. Pay attention to how your puppy reacts when people or other pets are nearby during meals. An anxious glance or a defensive stance may reveal discomfort, allowing you to address it before it becomes ingrained. By noticing these patterns, you can tailor your approach to suit your puppy's unique needs, beginning a positive feeding experience.

External and internal factors can significantly influence your puppy's approach to food. A stressful environment, such as loud noises or sudden changes in routine, can trigger anxiety, affecting their feeding behavior. Health issues, too, can play a role, with conditions like dental pain or digestive problems impacting appetite and demeanor. If your puppy's eating habits change suddenly, consider consulting a veterinarian to rule out medical concerns. A health check ensures that your puppy's behavior isn't a symptom of an underlying issue, allowing you to focus on behavioral adjustments confidently.

Reflection Section: Observing and Adjusting

Take a moment to reflect on your puppy's feeding habits. Ask yourself: what typical cues does your puppy display when comfortable or anxious during meals? How does your puppy react to different household members or pets approaching their food? Keeping a section in your journal to track these observations can help you understand your puppy's behavior more clearly, allowing you to make informed decisions about addressing any concerns. Adjust your approach based on these insights, ensuring your puppy's feeding routine supports their well-being and fosters a peaceful, trusting relationship.

Understanding these dynamics sets the stage for creating a harmonious feeding environment for your puppy. Addressing these natural instincts and external influences lays the foundation for a balanced, positive relationship with food, reducing the risk of aggression and ensuring calm, enjoyable mealtimes for everyone involved.

Implementing Safe Feeding Practices

Establishing a structured feeding routine is crucial for your puppy's well-being. It provides stability and predictability, reduces anxiety, and promotes healthy eating habits. Fixed meal times are the cornerstone of this routine. By feeding your puppy at the same time every day, you help them understand when to expect meals, which can alleviate any feelings of insecurity or hunger-driven anxiety. This predictability not only aids in digestion but also helps regulate your puppy's metabolism, ensuring they maintain a healthy weight. For households with multiple pets, separating feeding areas is important to prevent competition and potential conflicts. This separation allows each pet to enjoy their meal in peace, reducing the likelihood of resource guarding or aggressive behaviors.

Creating a calm feeding environment further supports your puppy's sense of security during mealtimes. Choose a quiet, low-traffic area of your home where your puppy can eat undisturbed. This space should be free from distractions, allowing your puppy to focus on their meal without feeling threatened or overwhelmed. Anti-slip mats under food and water bowls can add an extra layer of stability, preventing spills and keeping the bowls in place. This simple addition reduces the frustration of chasing a sliding bowl and helps your puppy enjoy their meal more comfortably. Setting up a peaceful feeding space reinforces the idea that mealtimes are safe, relaxed occasions, free from stress or competition.

Supervised feeding is an excellent way to build trust with your puppy while preventing the development of guarding behaviors. By staying nearby during meals, you reassure your puppy that they are safe and that you are a protector rather than a threat. It's essential to remain calm and avoid interfering with their eating process, as this can create unnecessary tension. Instead, offer quiet praise for calm behavior, reinforcing their confidence and comfort. Over time, your presence becomes a positive part of their mealtime routine, helping to prevent guarding instincts from taking root. This practice strengthens your bond with your puppy and sets the stage for peaceful, enjoyable meals in the future.

Interactive feeding tools are an excellent addition to your puppy's mealtime routine. They engage your puppy's mind, making eating a stimulating activity that enhances their well-being. Slow-feeder bowls are particularly effective in preventing gulping, a common issue that can lead to digestive problems. These bowls are designed with ridges or obstacles that encourage your puppy to eat more slowly, reducing the risk of choking or upset stomach. Puzzle feeders take engagement a step further by challenging your puppy to solve a puzzle to access their food. These feeders stimulate your puppy's natural curiosity and problem-solving skills, providing mental stimulation that can reduce boredom and prevent destructive behaviors.

These interactive tools make mealtimes more engaging and promote healthy eating habits. They encourage your puppy to savor their food, reducing the likelihood of overeating and supporting better digestion. Additionally, these tools can help manage weight by regulating portion sizes and preventing the rapid consumption of food. Incorporating these feeding tools into your puppy's routine provides both physical nourishment and mental enrichment, contributing to a balanced and fulfilling lifestyle. As your puppy grows and develops, these practices will play a vital role in their health and happiness, creating a lifelong appreciation for mealtime as a positive, rewarding experience.

An important consideration for your puppy's feeding schedule is the frequency of meals. Puppies, like infants, thrive on multiple small meals throughout the day. If your commitments only allow for morning and evening feedings, this interval may be too lengthy for your young pup, potentially leading to hunger and discomfort. To circumvent this, you could leave enough food accessible for your puppy to graze on throughout the day, ensuring they receive the necessary nutrition in your absence. Alternatively, enlisting the help of a friend, family member, or professional pet sitter to provide additional feedings can maintain your puppy's dietary routine until they mature and can adapt to fewer, more substantial meals.

Addressing and Correcting Food Guarding

You may notice subtle signs of food guarding as you watch your puppy during mealtimes. If left unchecked, these early indicators can escalate into more serious behaviors. One of the most common signs is a low growl or snap when someone approaches their food bowl. This vocal warning is a clear message from your puppy, signaling discomfort or possessiveness over their meal. In addition to vocal cues, pay attention to their body language. A stiffened posture or direct, unwavering stare can indicate that your puppy is on high alert. These physical signs are your puppy's way of communicating their unease or perceived threat; recognizing them early is the first step in addressing the issue.

Once you've identified food-guarding behavior, implementing gradual desensitization techniques can help reduce these instincts. Begin by standing at a comfortable distance from your puppy while they eat, gradually moving closer over several sessions. Pair your approach with positive outcomes, such as tossing a treat near their bowl while speaking softly and reassuringly. This method helps your puppy associate human presence with pleasant experiences rather than threats. Over time, your puppy will feel more relaxed when people are nearby during meals. This transformation doesn't happen overnight, so patience and persistence are essential. Every small step forward strengthens the bond of trust between you and your puppy, reinforcing the idea that mealtime is a safe and enjoyable experience.

In some cases, despite your best efforts, food guarding may persist or worsen. When this happens, seeking professional assistance can provide additional support and guidance. A certified dog trainer can offer strategies tailored to your puppy's needs. They bring a wealth of knowledge and experience, helping you and your puppy navigate this challenge. Consulting a professional is especially beneficial if your puppy's guarding behavior poses a risk to family members or other pets. Their expertise can help you manage the situation effectively, ensuring a harmonious and safe home environment for everyone.

Throughout this process, maintaining a calm, consistent approach is crucial. Avoid using punishment, as it can exacerbate aggression and increase anxiety. Instead, focus on celebrating small improvements and reinforcing positive behaviors. Each time your puppy allows you to approach without a defensive reaction, acknowledge their progress with praise or a treat. These moments of recognition motivate your puppy to continue making positive choices, fostering a sense of accomplishment and confidence. Remember that behavior modification takes time and effort, but the reward is a peaceful mealtime routine and a stronger relationship with your puppy.

It's important to remember that understanding and addressing food guarding is just one aspect of nurturing a well-rounded, confident dog. By recognizing early signs and implementing effective strategies, you create a foundation of trust and respect. This journey is about more than just correcting behavior; it's about building a lifelong connection with your puppy, where they feel safe and secure.

Teaching "Leave It" and "Wait" Commands

Imagine your puppy in a bustling park, surrounded by distractions—other dogs, people, and enticing scents. In such a setting, the "Leave It" and "Wait" commands become invaluable tools. These commands are not just about obedience; they lay the groundwork for impulse control and respect. Instilling these commands early on can prevent impulsive reactions that may lead to aggression. "Leave It" teaches your puppy to resist the urge to grab or guard items, promoting calmness and control. Meanwhile, the "Wait" command encourages patience, especially before meals, when excitement might otherwise lead to anxious behaviors. These commands help your puppy understand boundaries, fostering a sense of respect for you and your surroundings.

Teaching "Leave It." Start with a low-value item, perhaps a piece of kibble, and place it on the floor. As your puppy approaches, cover it with your hand and firmly say, "Leave it." When your puppy stops trying to get the item and looks away, reward them with a high-value treat and praise. Consistent success with this basic exercise means it's time to increase the difficulty. Introduce more enticing items, always rewarding your puppy for obeying the command. Consistency is key. Each time your puppy follows through, reinforce their success with a treat, gradually reducing the frequency of rewards as their understanding solidifies. This approach strengthens your puppy's impulse control, reducing the likelihood of aggression over-valued items.

Teaching "Wait." This is equally vital and can be seamlessly integrated into your daily routine. Utilize meal times as practice opportunities. Hold your puppy's food bowl and ask them to "Wait." If they remain calm, gradually lower the bowl. Should your puppy leap forward, lift the bowl back up and try again, rewarding patience with their meal. Over time, increase the waiting period before giving the release cue, "Okay," allowing them to eat. This method helps your puppy associate patience with positive outcomes, reinforcing the importance of self-control. Consistent practice during feeding times makes the "Wait" command a natural part of your puppy's daily life, promoting calm behavior and reducing anxiety.

Commands like "Leave It" and "Wait" are not limited to structured training sessions. Incorporate them into everyday scenarios to reinforce their importance and maintain your puppy's focus. Use "Leave It" during walks when passing distracting items or other dogs, rewarding compliance with a treat. This strengthens the command and enhances your puppy's ability to concentrate amidst distractions. Similarly, "Wait" can be practiced during playtime. Ask your puppy to "Wait" before chasing a toy, releasing them with "Okay." This reinforces patience and obedience, even in high-energy situations. By weaving these commands into daily life, you create a consistent framework for your puppy, helping them navigate the world with confidence and respect.

Teaching these commands requires patience and consistency. Celebrate small victories and remain calm during setbacks. Each successful execution of "Leave It" or "Wait" builds your puppy's confidence and understanding, reinforcing the bond between you. Engage family members in practicing these commands, ensuring consistent reinforcement across different environments. As your puppy masters these skills, you'll notice a marked improvement in their impulse control and respect for boundaries, creating a harmonious living environment for you both. Next, we'll explore the vital role of socialization in your puppy's development, ensuring they grow into a well-adjusted and sociable companion.

Your Experience Can Help Another Puppy Parent

Bringing a puppy home is a journey filled with excitement, learning, and a few surprises along the way. Every puppy parent wants the best for their furry companion, and sometimes, the right guidance can make all the difference.

Would you please take a moment to help someone just like you—someone eager to train their puppy but unsure where to start?

Our mission with *Puppy Training Bible, 6 Simple Steps* is to make training easy, effective, and enjoyable for everyone. But to reach more people, we need your help.

Why Your Review Matters

Most people choose books based on reviews. By sharing your experience, you're not just leaving feedback—you're helping another dog owner build a better bond with their puppy. Your review could mean...

> 🐾 **One more puppy feeling safe and confident in their home.**
> 🐾 **One more busy owner experiencing stress-free, enjoyable training.**
> 🐾 **One more family creating lifelong memories with their well-trained dog.**
> 🐾 **One more rescue dog getting a second chance with the right guidance.**

It costs nothing and takes less than a minute, but your words could make a world of difference for someone on this same journey. If this book has helped you, please pass it forward. Your insight can guide another puppy owner toward success.

Thank you for being part of this journey, Trinity Wood Press

Leave a Review in Just One Click: To go directly to the review page, simply **scan the QR code below** or click this link to share your thoughts:

👉 https://www.amazon.com/review/review-your-purchases/?asin=B0F6YRXHZ5

Leave a Review

Chapter 6

Step Four: Socializing Your Puppy

As you step into puppy parenthood, you soon realize that your little furball is more than just a bundle of energy and curiosity. They are sponges, absorbing every sight, sound, and experience. This stage of life, particularly between 3 and 14 weeks, is a pivotal time for socialization. During this critical window, your puppy's encounters shape their future behavior and personality. The experiences they gather now will influence how they respond to the world as adults. Proper socialization during this period can prevent future behavioral problems such as fear and aggression, setting the stage for a well-adjusted, confident dog.

Understanding the timing of socialization is crucial. While you may be eager to introduce your puppy to new experiences, it's essential to consider their vaccination schedule. Your veterinarian can help guide you on when it's safe to begin exposing your puppy to public places. Until vaccinations are underway, focus on controlled environments that minimize disease risk. This balance ensures that your puppy gains exposure without compromising their health. Early socialization impacts your puppy's comfort with different situations and plays a role in their overall health and well-being. In my experience, many new puppy owners eagerly anticipate taking their new puppies to parks or around town. Unfortunately, some are not fully aware of the risk's young puppies face from diseases, which can be severe and even life-threatening. A prime example is Canine Parvovirus, more commonly known as parvo, a highly contagious viral disease that poses a significant risk to dogs, especially puppies, who have not yet built a robust immune system. Puppies can contract parvo in several ways.

Direct contact with infected dog or feces in public areas: Transmission can occur through interaction with an infected dog's saliva, vomit, or feces—contaminated *surfaces or objects*. The parvovirus can linger on surfaces and objects for long periods. Puppies can become infected by contacting contaminated items, such as toys, food bowls, or bedding. *Inhalation:* Although rare, the virus can be transmitted through the air if an infected dog coughs or sneezes in proximity. Puppies are particularly susceptible to parvo, given their developing immune systems, but unvaccinated adult dogs are also at risk. This underscores the importance of caution and prioritizing vaccinations before exposing puppies to broader public settings.

After proper vaccinations, you can begin your introduction to the world by starting with low-stress environments. Initially, this would mean interactions within your home or yard. But gradually, you can broaden their experiences to include more complex settings. Pair these experiences with treats and praise, reinforcing positive feelings and building your puppy's confidence. The goal is to create a positive association with each new experience, encouraging curiosity and adaptability. Doing so, you help your puppy develop the resilience needed to navigate various situations calmly and confidently.

Varied environments play a significant role in developing your puppy's adaptability. Exposing them to different settings—from the serenity of a park to the hustle and bustle of urban life—teaches them to adapt to diverse circumstances. This variety helps your puppy learn to cope with different stimuli, reducing the likelihood of developing anxiety in unfamiliar situations. Walking on various surfaces, such as grass, sand, and pavement, introduces your puppy to new textures underfoot, broadening their comfort zone. These environments challenge your puppy to process and adapt to new sensory inputs, strengthening their ability to remain calm and composed in varied settings.

Monitoring your puppy's comfort level throughout this socialization process is important. Pay close attention to their reactions; they'll communicate their feelings through body language and behavior. Adjust the pace if your puppy seems overwhelmed—perhaps they're hesitating, cowering, or showing signs of stress. Slow down, and give them time to acclimate. Use calming techniques to reassure them. This might include stepping away from the stimulus, speaking softly, or offering comfort through touch or treats. The key is to respect your puppy's limits, ensuring that each experience is a positive step forward rather than a source of stress.

Reflection Section: Socialization Progress Journal

Note the environments they visit, their reactions, and any triggers that cause stress or excitement. Consider keeping a section in your journal to track your puppy's socialization experiences. Reflect on the following: How did your puppy respond to a new setting today? Were there any signs of discomfort or fear? What positive reinforcements did you use, and how did they affect your puppy's behavior? Documenting these experiences helps you tailor future socialization efforts and provides a valuable record of your puppy's growth and development. This practice encourages an ongoing dialogue between you and your puppy, fostering a deeper understanding and a stronger bond.

Introducing Your Puppy to New People and Pets

Introducing your puppy to new people is a delightful yet delicate process that lays the foundation for their social skills. Start by encouraging gentle handling and respectful interactions. This means guiding friends and family to approach your puppy calmly, avoiding sudden movements that might startle them. Kneel to their level, offering a hand for them to sniff before attempting to pet. This small gesture lets your puppy feel safe and in control of the encounter. Reward your puppy's calm behavior during these greetings with treats or soothing praise, reinforcing that meeting new people is a positive experience. Each interaction should be brief and pleasant, ensuring your puppy doesn't feel overwhelmed.

Diverse interactions are crucial in preventing future fear and aggression. By exposing your puppy to various people, you help them become well-rounded and adaptable. Introduce them to individuals of different ages, ethnicities, and attire. A child in a bright jacket, an older person with a cane, or someone wearing a hat—all these encounters help your puppy learn that people come in many forms and are not to be feared. Similarly, exposure to other animals is beneficial. Start with well-behaved adult dogs, cats, or even smaller pets like rabbits. These interactions teach your puppy the nuances of different species and temperaments, building their confidence in social situations. Always supervise these meetings to ensure they remain safe and positive, stepping in if any party becomes uncomfortable.

Puppy play dates are another excellent way to socialize your puppy with their peers. Organize small group play sessions with other vaccinated puppies or adult dogs. Choose a neutral, enclosed space where the dogs can interact freely but safely. Monitor the play closely to prevent rough behavior or bullying—puppies can get carried away in their excitement. If one puppy seems too dominant or another appears stressed, gently intervene to restore balance. These play dates allow your puppy to develop critical social skills, such as reading body language and learning appropriate play behavior. They also provide physical exercise and mental stimulation, contributing to your puppy's overall well-being.

Enrolling your puppy in a socialization class provides structured learning through supervised play and professional guidance. These classes are designed to expose puppies to various experiences in a controlled environment. Trainers offer valuable insights into your puppy's behavior, helping you address any emerging issues early on. Classes typically include activities challenging your puppy's mind and body, from basic obedience to agility exercises. The presence of other puppies allows your dog to learn how to interact in a group setting, developing patience and turn-taking. Socialization classes also allow you to connect with other puppy parents, sharing experiences and tips for successful training.

The benefits of these classes extend beyond the immediate socialization. They lay the groundwork for future learning and cooperation, making subsequent training easier. The skills your puppy acquires in class, such as following commands and focusing amidst distractions, are invaluable. They foster a sense of achievement and confidence in your puppy, positively impacting their behavior at home and in public. With each new person and pet your puppy meets, they build a range of experiences that enrich their understanding of the world. This diversity in social interactions is key to raising a well-adjusted, comfortable, confident dog.

Navigating Public Spaces with Confidence

Taking your puppy into public spaces allows them to learn about the world around them. Once vaccinations have started and your vet says your puppy is protected, start with positive exposure to different environments by visiting dog-friendly stores or outdoor cafés. These spots tend to be bustling with activity yet offer a controlled setting where you can maintain oversight. Initially, observe busy streets from a safe distance, allowing your puppy to acclimate to the noise and movement. As they grow more comfortable, you can gradually move closer. This slow introduction helps your puppy become accustomed to the sights and sounds they'll encounter in everyday life, making future outings less daunting.

Leash training serves as the cornerstone for successful public outings. A well-trained puppy on a leash is easier to manage and keeps both of you safe. Before progressing to busier areas, begin by practicing controlled leash walking in varied environments, such as quiet neighborhoods or empty parks. Using treats or verbal praise, is crucial in positive reinforcement and maintaining your puppy's focus and calm. Whenever they walk nicely beside you, reward them with a treat and a kind word. This encourages your puppy to associate good behavior with positive outcomes, enhancing their willingness to cooperate.

Introducing new stimuli gradually is key to preventing your puppy from becoming overwhelmed. Begin with moderate noises like distant traffic or the chatter of people at a café. As your puppy becomes more confident, introduce them to louder or more complex sounds, such as sirens or children playing. Pay close attention to how your puppy reacts to these new experiences. If they show signs of stress or discomfort, such as pulling back on the leash or trying to hide, take a step back and give them time to adjust. This approach respects your puppy's comfort level while gradually broadening their experiences.

Distractions are inevitable in public spaces, but with the right strategies, you can help your puppy maintain focus and composure. High-value treats are excellent for capturing your puppy's attention amidst distractions. Keep these treats handy and offer them as a reward for good behavior, such as walking calmly past another dog or sitting quietly at your feet while you chat with a friend. Practicing basic commands like "sit" or "stay" in these settings further reinforces their training, demonstrating to your puppy that listening to you is rewarding. These commands not only keep your puppy engaged but also provide them with a sense of security, knowing what to expect in different situations.

Navigating public spaces with your puppy is a gradual process that requires patience and consistency. Each outing is a learning experience, allowing your puppy to grow more comfortable and confident. By taking the time to introduce new environments and stimuli thoughtfully, you help your puppy develop into a well-rounded and adaptable dog. These experiences enrich their understanding of the world and strengthen the bond between you, paving the way for a lifetime of enjoyable adventures together.

Managing Overexcitement and Fear

Puppies are bundles of energy and emotions; sometimes, they don't quite know how to control it all. Recognizing the signs of overexcitement and fear is your first step in guiding them towards calmness and confidence. Overexcited puppies often jump, bark, and wag their tails furiously. They might dart around the room, unable to settle. It's like they've had a sugar rush and don't know how to come down. On the flip side, fear can manifest as tail tucking, cowering, or even trembling. Your puppy might flatten themselves against the ground or try to hide behind your legs. These cues are their way of communicating discomfort or uncertainty in their environment.

When your puppy is overexcited, channeling that energy is key. Redirect their attention to a favorite toy or treat. This distracts them and provides a way for them to focus on something positive. Engaging them in calming exercises can also help. Simple commands like "sit" or "down" can work wonders in helping your puppy regain composure. These exercises divert their energy and reinforce obedience, providing a momentary pause that allows your puppy to reset. In time, they learn that moments of calmness bring rewards, encouraging them to self-regulate.

Fear, on the other hand, requires a different approach. Building your puppy's confidence in stressful situations involves gradual desensitization to the fear-inducing stimulus. Introduce the scary object or sound at a distance or low intensity, pairing it with treats and praise. Move slowly, allowing your puppy to approach at their own pace. This process teaches them they are safe, even when confronted with something new or intimidating. It's equally important to provide a safe retreat space, like a crate or a cozy bed. This sanctuary offers your puppy a place to retreat when the world becomes too overwhelming, reinforcing their sense of security.

Building resilience in your puppy is an ongoing process that supports their emotional growth. Introduce new challenges in controlled settings, where you can monitor their reactions and offer support. Whether it's a new toy, a visit to a different part of the house, or a short car ride, these experiences build adaptability. Each time your puppy faces a challenge and emerges unscathed, their confidence grows. Rewarding brave behavior with treats or affection boosts their self-assurance, teaching them that courage brings positive outcomes. This resilience will serve them well throughout life, equipping them to handle change gracefully.

In your journey of socializing your puppy, you've equipped them with the tools to navigate excitement and fear. By understanding their emotions and guiding them with patience, you lay the foundation for a confident and adaptable adult dog. As you continue to nurture this growth, you'll find that each new experience further enriches your bond. With these skills in hand, your puppy is ready to face the adventures that await in the next section, where we'll explore essential commands that will cement your training and deepen your connection.

Chapter 7

Step Five: Teaching Recall

Teaching your puppy to come when called is not just a convenient skill—it's a critical component of their safety and your peace of mind. A reliable recall means your puppy will respond with eagerness and confidence no matter the distraction.

A reliable recall is more than a command; it's a testament to the trust and understanding between you and your puppy. When your puppy learns to come when called, they recognize you as a source of safety and assurance. This trust is built through consistent and positive reinforcement, creating a stronger bond with each successful recall. As your puppy returns to you, they experience a sense of security in knowing that you're their anchor, ready to guide and protect them. This relationship fosters an environment where learning becomes a shared adventure of encouragement and support.

Turning recall into a game can make training engaging and enjoyable for you and your puppy. One effective method is to play hide-and-seek. Begin by hiding in a familiar area and calling your puppy's name with a cheerful tone. When they find you, shower them with praise and a treat. This game reinforces the recall command and stimulates your puppy's natural instincts to seek and find. Another approach is to use their favorite toy as a reward for successful recall. Toss the toy, and call them back with enthusiasm as your puppy retrieves it. The joy of play combined with the reward reinforces the behavior, making recall a delightful experience.

Start with short distances in a distraction-free area to lay the groundwork for recall training. This controlled environment ensures your puppy focuses on you and is free from external stimuli. Use a light, happy tone to call them, making the command inviting rather than authoritative. The tone should convey excitement and positivity, encouraging your puppy to respond with the same enthusiasm. As they trot toward you, welcome them with open arms and a treat, reinforcing that coming to you is always a rewarding choice. These initial steps form the basis of a recall command that your puppy will associate with positive experiences.

Consistency and repetition are the basis of effective recall training. Scheduling daily practice sessions helps solidify the skills your puppy learns, ensuring they become second nature. Regular practice reinforces the behavior and builds your puppy's confidence in understanding and executing the command. As your puppy becomes more proficient, gradually increase the difficulty level by introducing mild distractions or extending the distance. This progression challenges your puppy to maintain focus and recall ability in varied circumstances, preparing them for real-world scenarios. By consistently applying these principles, you create a framework where recall becomes an instinctual response, strengthening the trust and connection between you and your puppy.

Training recall effectively demands patience and dedication, but the rewards are immeasurable. Regardless of the situation, the joy of seeing your puppy respond eagerly to your call underscores the strength of the bond you've cultivated. This section isn't merely about teaching a command; it's about fostering a relationship built on trust, respect, and mutual understanding. As you integrate recall training into your routine, you'll find it enriches your puppy's life and your own, enhancing the joy and freedom you share together.

Reflection Section: Recall Practice Journal

Consider keeping a recall practice section in your journal to track your puppy's progress. Record each session, noting the environment, distance, and response time. Reflect on what worked well and what might need adjustment. This journal becomes a valuable tool in refining your approach, ensuring your puppy continues to thrive in their recall training journey.

Positive Reinforcement for Recall Success

Positive reinforcement is an incredibly effective tool in recall training, transforming the "come" command into an exciting invitation rather than a chore. Imagine your puppy racing toward you enthusiastically, fueled by the knowledge that a reward awaits. This technique increases the likelihood of your puppy obeying the recall command and enhances your bond. High-value treats play a pivotal role here. These aren't your everyday kibble; they're special rewards that appeal significantly to your puppy. Think of small pieces of chicken or cheese—something your puppy doesn't always get. The aroma and taste of these treats make them irresistible, serving as a powerful motivator for your puppy to respond quickly and eagerly. Alongside these treats, verbal praise and physical affection are crucial. A cheerful "Good job!" and a gentle pat or belly rub reinforce your puppy's positive behavior. This combination of rewards strengthens the recall response, making your puppy associate coming a delightful outcome.

Timing is everything in recall training. The moment your puppy reaches you, that's when you reward them. Immediate rewards are essential because they help your puppy connect the behavior with the treat. If there's a delay, your puppy might not make the connection, weakening the impact of the training. As soon as your puppy arrives, offer the treat and lavish praise. This immediate response reinforces that coming to you is an excellent decision. Maintaining consistency over time is crucial for ingraining it into your puppy's behavior, ensuring it becomes a reliable action.

Consistent and timely rewards build a strong foundation for recall training, ensuring your puppy understands the positive consequences of their actions.

To keep your puppy engaged, varying the rewards is key. Imagine a world where every treat is the same—monotony would soon set in, diminishing your puppy's enthusiasm. You maintain your puppy's interest and motivation by rotating between different rewards. One day, you might offer a tasty treat; the next, a quick game of fetch or tug-of-war. Occasionally, a few moments of playtime can be just as rewarding as a treat, especially for puppies that thrive on interaction. This variety prevents predictability, keeping your puppy guessing and eager to respond. The anticipation of what reward might come next encourages your puppy to participate actively, reinforcing recall behavior with each successful attempt.

As your puppy becomes more consistent in their recall, it's time to gradually wean them off constant treat rewards. Transitioning to praise-only rewards involves careful consideration. Start by occasionally replacing treats with enthusiastic praise and affection, showing your puppy that your approval is valuable. Gradually increase the frequency of praise-only rewards while still offering treats intermittently. This approach helps your puppy learn that rewards come in many forms and that the joy of pleasing you is a reward in itself.

Additionally, implementing a variable reward schedule maintains responsiveness. By varying when and how often rewards are given, you keep the training dynamic and engaging. Your puppy won't know when the next treat will appear, keeping them attentive and eager to respond whenever you call.

Incorporating positive reinforcement into recall training transforms the entire process into a rewarding experience for you and your puppy. Combining high-value treats, timely rewards, and varied incentives ensures your puppy remains excited and engaged, eager to respond to the recall command. This approach strengthens the behavior and deepens the bond between you and your puppy, fostering a relationship built on trust, respect, and shared joy. By consistently applying these principles, recall training becomes enjoyable and fulfilling, laying the groundwork for a lifetime of companionship and adventure.

Practicing Recall in Varied Environments

In a controlled setting, you'll start with recall practice, your voice commanding their attention as you call them to you. Free of distractions, this setting is ideal for reinforcing the basics before venturing out to more challenging territories. Once your puppy masters recall in this safe space, it's time to introduce new environments with unique distractions and challenges. A quiet park might be your next step, where the occasional bird or passerby tests your puppy's focus. As their confidence grows, introduce them to more bustling environments, such as active parks, where they can practice their recall against diverse distractions.

Distractions are part and parcel of any outdoor adventure, and maintaining your puppy's attention becomes the key challenge. A long leash or line can be a fantastic tool, allowing your puppy to explore while keeping them safely tethered. This gives you control over situations that might otherwise lead to a chase. Alongside this, practicing commands like "watch me" draws their attention back to you, reinforcing that amidst all the excitement, you're the most interesting thing around. This command helps keep their focus and strengthens your bond as they learn to look to you for guidance and reassurance.

As your puppy becomes more adept at returning to you, the distance over which you practice recall can slowly increase. Imagine calling your puppy from across the yard, then gradually extending that distance until they come to you from the other side of a field. This incremental increase helps them understand that the recall command applies, no matter how far they wander. Enlisting a helper can add an extra dimension to this training. Have someone hold your puppy as you walk away, then call them to you. This builds anticipation and reinforces the idea that even when separated, they should come when called.

Variety enhances recall training, making it adaptable to noisy environments where your voice might not stand out. Alternative signals like a sharp whistle, a distinct clap, or hand signals can be invaluable. These methods ensure your commands cut through ambient noise, capturing your puppy's attention. Starting recall training in a distraction-free, familiar environment like your backyard sets a solid foundation. As your puppy masters the basics, gradually introduce more complex settings with varying levels of distractions, such as quiet parks, progressing to busier ones. This step-by-step increase in difficulty boosts your puppy's confidence and sharpens their focus amidst distractions. Utilizing tools like a long leash can allow your puppy to explore while ensuring their safety, reinforcing that you are the focal point of interest and security. Incrementally extending the recall distance and incorporating helpers for training can enhance your puppy's responsiveness, building anticipation and understanding that they should return to you, regardless of the situation. Introducing various recall cues—verbal commands, whistles, claps, or hand signals—adds a layer of flexibility and reliability to your training, ensuring your puppy can adapt and respond in any setting. This approach improves recall effectiveness and enriches the training experience, fostering a deeper bond and mutual trust between you and your puppy as you explore new environments.

In varied environments, recall training becomes an adventure, a chance to explore new places with your puppy while reinforcing vital skills. Each setting offers its own lessons, teaching your puppy to concentrate and respond amidst the hustle and bustle of the outside world. As you practice across different landscapes, you'll notice your puppy's recall improving, their eagerness to return to you sharpening with each session. It's a testament to the trust and understanding you've built, a relationship strengthened by every call answered and every race back to your side.

Overcoming Recall Challenges

Recall training can sometimes hit a few bumps along the road, and recognizing these obstacles is the first step to overcoming them. Often, the world is a captivating place for a puppy, filled with numerous distractions that can easily steal their attention. Whether it's the rustling of leaves, the scent of another dog, or the distant sounds of people, these stimuli can make your command feel less appealing. This disinterest doesn't mean your puppy is intentionally ignoring you; it's simply a natural response to their environment. Another hurdle could be fear or anxiety, particularly if your puppy has had negative experiences in the past. A loud noise or an intimidating situation can make them hesitant to respond, as their focus shifts to self-protection rather than obedience. Understanding these challenges allows you to approach training with empathy and patience, setting a foundation for success.

When you notice reluctance in your puppy's recall, it's time to reevaluate and adapt your approach. One effective strategy is to heighten the allure of your rewards, especially in settings where distractions abound. Imagine offering your puppy a piece of chicken instead of standard kibble when calling them back from a particularly enticing distraction. The key is to make your reward more appealing than the surrounding environment. Additionally, practicing recall over shorter distances can help rebuild your puppy's confidence. By calling them from just a few steps away, you create a situation where success is almost guaranteed. Gradually, as their confidence grows, you can increase the distance again. This method helps your puppy associate the recall command with positive outcomes, reinforcing their willingness to follow through. These adjustments create an environment where your puppy feels motivated and secure.

Patience and perseverance are your greatest allies in recall training. It's easy to feel frustrated when your puppy seems uninterested or hesitant, but maintaining a calm and positive demeanor is crucial. Frustration can inadvertently create a negative association with the command, making your puppy even more resistant. Instead, approach each session with a fresh perspective, acknowledging small victories along the way. Celebrate the moments when your puppy responds correctly, and use them as building blocks for future success. Remember, training is not a race; it's a series of steps that take time and dedication. With each attempt, you're teaching a command and strengthening your bond with your puppy.

There are times when, despite your best efforts, recall challenges persist. In these cases, seeking professional help can provide additional support and guidance. A qualified dog trainer can offer tailored advice, drawing from their experience to address specific issues you might face. They can observe your interactions with your puppy and suggest personalized strategies to improve recall. This professional insight can be invaluable, especially if your puppy's reluctance stems from deep-seated fear or anxiety. Having an expert by your side not only aids in resolving challenges but also boosts your confidence as a trainer. It's a collaborative effort to ensure your puppy's success in mastering recall.

As you continue with recall training, remember that every step forward, no matter how small, is progress. The process might be slow, but these improvements lead to lasting results. With patience, adaptability, and the right support, your puppy will learn to respond confidently and eagerly to your call. This section on recall training is not merely about teaching a command; it's about building trust, understanding, and communication between you and your puppy. With this foundation, you pave the way for a lifetime of shared adventures and joyful companionship.

Chapter 8

Step Six: Leash Walking

You'll soon enjoy the thrill of stepping out on a crisp morning with your eager puppy at your side, ready to explore the world together. Leash walking is not just a routine; it's an adventure filled with new sights, sounds, and experiences. But before you set off, choosing the right leash and collar sets the foundation for a safe and enjoyable journey. The equipment you select impacts both training and safety. Standard leashes, often made of nylon or leather, offer durability and a steady grip, making them an excellent choice for training. They provide a controlled environment where you can guide your puppy gently, teaching them to walk calmly beside you.

In contrast, while popular for giving dogs more freedom, retractable leashes can present challenges. They often encourage pulling as puppies learn to extend their range by tugging harder. This can inadvertently teach undesirable behaviors, especially in young dogs still learning boundaries.

Regarding collars, the options are as varied as the dogs that wear them. Flat collars are the most common, serving as a simple tool for identification and control. They work well for puppies that walk nicely on a leash without pulling. However, a martingale collar might be more suitable for those in training or prone to pulling. These collars provide a gentle correction by tightening slightly when the puppy pulls, discouraging the behavior without obstructing the airway. Harnesses offer another alternative. They distribute pressure across the chest and shoulders, reducing strain on the neck. Harnesses come in various styles, from simple step-ins to more intricate designs with adjustable straps for a perfect fit. While harnesses are beneficial for distributing pressure and reducing neck strain, they may not always offer the same level of control as a martingale collar for a puppy that pulls. No-pull harnesses would be another excellent option, designed to reduce pulling by attaching the leash at the chest. Ultimately, finding the most effective tool depends on observing how your puppy responds and choosing the best option for their learning and safety.

Ensuring the collar and leash fit properly is crucial to prevent discomfort or injury. A collar that's too tight can cause chafing or restrict breathing, while one that's too loose might slip off. To find the right fit, measure your puppy's neck and add a couple of inches to ensure comfort. You should be able to slip two fingers between the collar and your puppy's neck. With harnesses, pay attention to how they sit on your puppy's body. Adjust the straps to avoid chafing or slipping, ensuring your puppy can move comfortably without restriction. This attention to fit enhances comfort and boosts your puppy's confidence during walks, knowing their gear is secure and supportive.

Training aids can be invaluable allies in the journey to leash walking mastery. Head halters, for instance, offer additional control by guiding your puppy's head, similar to a horse's halter. This can be particularly useful for strong, energetic puppies that tend to pull ahead. This encourages your puppy to walk beside you rather than forging ahead, making walks more enjoyable for both of you. When used correctly, these tools enhance communication between you and your puppy, facilitating a smoother training experience.

The choice of materials for your leash and collar is a balance between comfort and durability. Nylon is a popular choice, known for its affordability and resilience. It's especially suitable for growing puppies, as it can withstand the wear and tear of their exuberant explorations. Leather offers elegance and strength, molding to your puppy's neck over time for a custom fit. While it requires more maintenance, leather's longevity and classic appeal make it a worthwhile investment. Reflective materials are an excellent addition to any leash or collar, enhancing visibility during night walks or in low-light conditions. They provide an extra layer of safety, ensuring you and your puppy are seen by passing vehicles or pedestrians.

Reflection Section: Gear Assessment Checklist

- *Leash Style: Decide between a standard or retractable leash based on your training goals.*
- *Collar Type: Choose flat, martingale, or harness based on your puppy's size and behavior.*
- *Fit and Comfort: Ensure collars and harnesses are snug but comfortable, with room for two fingers.*
- *Training Aids: Consider head halters or no-pull harnesses if your puppy tends to pull.*
- *Material Choice: Opt for nylon for durability or leather for a classic touch; don't forget reflective elements for safety.*

Selecting the right leash and collar is more than a simple purchase; it's an investment in your puppy's safety and training success. With the right gear, every walk becomes an opportunity to build trust, reinforce training, and enjoy the simple pleasures of exploring together.

Introducing Your Puppy to Leash Walking

Start by letting your puppy wear the leash indoors where they feel safe and familiar. Attach the leash without any pressure to walk or perform. Allow them to drag it around for short periods so they get used to its presence. This simple act helps the leash become just another part of their environment, not something to be feared. As your puppy moves around on the leash, encourage them with soft words and treats, reinforcing the idea that this is a positive experience. Ensure you closely watch that they don't start chewing on the leash as if it were a toy to prevent the formation of any undesirable habits from the beginning.

Creating positive associations with the leash is important in building your puppy's confidence. Each time you attach the leash, offer a treat and a kind word. This simple routine can make all the difference in how your puppy perceives leash time. Start with short, positive sessions, perhaps just a few minutes at first, gradually increasing as your puppy becomes more comfortable. These brief interactions help build their confidence and reinforce that wearing a leash leads to fun and rewards. Over time, your puppy will begin to associate the leash with enjoyable outings and quality time with you, transforming what could be a daunting process into a delightful one.

Practicing leash walking indoors is an excellent way to minimize distractions and focus on building the basics. Begin by walking your puppy on the leash in a familiar space, like your living room or hallway. These controlled environments allow you to practice fundamental skills such as turns and stops, which are essential for coordination and communication between you and your puppy. Use treats to guide your puppy through these motions, rewarding them for staying by your side. This indoor practice lays the groundwork for more complex outdoor environments, ensuring your puppy feels secure and confident before going into the big outdoors. It's a low-pressure way for both of you to learn and adapt.

Patience and gradual exposure are your best friends when introducing your puppy to leash walking. It's tempting to jump into long walks immediately, but starting slowly helps build a strong foundation. Increase the duration of walks gradually, paying attention to your puppy's comfort and energy levels. Allow them to explore and sniff during walks, turning each outing into an adventure filled with new experiences and scents. This exploration is enjoyable for your puppy and stimulates their mind, contributing to their overall development. By progressing at a pace comfortable for your puppy, you foster a sense of security and trust that will last a lifetime.

Remember that every step, no matter how small, contributes to a lifetime of enjoyable walks together. This stage is about more than just training; it's about building a bond based on trust and positive reinforcement. Each walk becomes a chance to strengthen your relationship, explore the world, and create shared memories. With patience, encouragement, and a touch of creativity, you'll find that leash walking becomes a natural and cherished part of your daily routine.

Addressing Pulling and Lunging on Leash

Leash walking with a puppy sometimes feels like a tug-of-war rather than a peaceful stroll. Puppies often pull or lunge due to an abundance of excitement and curiosity. Seeing another dog or a friendly stranger can be utterly irresistible, prompting them to dart forward with all their might. This eagerness to engage with new friends is normal but must be managed to prevent it from becoming a habit. Sometimes, it isn't just excitement; fear or anxiety can spur sudden movements. A loud noise or unfamiliar sight might trigger your puppy to bolt toward or away from the source. Understanding these triggers is the first step in addressing the behavior.

You can use the "stop and go" method to teach your puppy to walk calmly beside you. This simple technique involves stopping in your tracks whenever your puppy begins to pull on the leash. By standing still and waiting for your puppy to return their focus to you, you send a clear message: pulling doesn't get you anywhere. Once the leash is slack and your puppy's attention is back on you, give a gentle command to continue, rewarding them with a treat or praise. Over time, your puppy will learn that maintaining a relaxed demeanor keeps the walk moving forward while pulling only halts the adventure.

Reinforcing loose leash walking with treats can transform your outings. Keep some high-value treats handy, and reward your puppy whenever they walk beside you with the leash slack. This positive reinforcement encourages good behavior and makes the walk more enjoyable for both of you. By consistently rewarding your puppy for walking calmly, you're teaching them that sticking close by is beneficial and rewarding. The consistency of this approach helps cement the desired behavior, fostering a sense of partnership as you explore the world together.

Redirecting your puppy's focus away from distractions can be a game-changer. The "look at me" command is a great tool for this. Practice this command in a distraction-free environment by holding a treat near your face and saying, "Look at me." When your puppy makes eye contact, reward them with the treat. Gradually introduce more distractions as your puppy improves, using the command to regain their attention when needed. Additionally, carrying a favorite toy can help redirect your puppy's focus when something catches their eye. Offering the toy or treat as you pass a potential distraction can help keep their attention on you.

Consistent practice and positive reinforcement are crucial in developing good leash habits. Schedule daily leash training sessions, even if they're short. Consistency helps reinforce what your puppy has learned, turning new skills into second nature. Celebrate each small success with praise and rewards, strengthening the bond between you and your puppy. As you make progress, remember that setbacks are normal. Patience and persistence will pave the way for a lifetime of enjoyable walks together. Each outing becomes an opportunity to learn and grow, transforming what once felt like a struggle into an experience of connection and joy.

Safe Tie-Out Practices

Recognizing that many owners may not have a fenced-in area, I feel it's essential to address safe tie-out practices. Without access to a fenced-in yard, tie-outs can be a practical solution for giving your puppy some freedom while ensuring their safety. These devices allow your puppy to explore the outdoors without the confines of a fenced yard. Thou their use comes with important considerations. On the one hand, tie-outs allow your dog to play and roam in a controlled manner, keeping them secure within a specific radius. This can be beneficial when camping or on picnics, where you want your puppy to enjoy the outdoors without wandering too far.

On the other hand, using tie-outs requires vigilance. Puppies can quickly become tangled, leading to panic or even injury if they try to free themselves. Additionally, without proper supervision, there's a risk of escape if the tie-out isn't securely fastened or if the puppy manages to slip out of their collar or harness. Therefore, understanding both the advantages and risks of tie-outs is crucial to using them effectively and safely.

Selecting an appropriate location for your tie-out is as important as the equipment. Choose an area free of obstacles and hazards that could cause your puppy to become entangled. Look for open spaces where your puppy can move freely, away from trees, furniture, or any objects they might wrap their tie-out around. It's also important to consider environmental factors. Ensure they have access to shade and water to prevent overheating or dehydration. This consideration is especially crucial on hot days, where the risk of heatstroke is heightened. By carefully choosing the location, you create a safer environment that allows your puppy to enjoy their playtime outside without unnecessary risks.

The right equipment and secure installation are important when setting up a tie-out. Use sturdy stakes that anchor firmly into the ground and swivel clips that provide flexibility without the risk of tangling. The tie-out length should offer enough freedom for your puppy to move and play but not so much that it becomes a hazard. A good rule of thumb is to ensure the tie-out is long enough for a comfortable radius and short enough to prevent reaching potential dangers. Proper tie-out system installation and maintenance are essential to providing your puppy with a safe and enjoyable experience.

Supervision and monitoring are non-negotiable when using a tie-out. Always keep your puppy within sight, ready to intervene if they encounter an issue. Regularly inspect the tie-out, checking for signs of wear and ensuring it remains securely anchored. This vigilance is especially important if your puppy is active or prone to chewing. You can quickly address problems by staying attentive, preventing minor issues from becoming major safety concerns. Remember, tie-outs are not a substitute for attention and should only be used when you can keep an eye on your puppy. This ensures your puppy's safety and allows them to enjoy their outdoor playtime to the fullest.

As we wrap up our exploration of leash walking and tie-out safety, it's clear that preparation and vigilance are key. Choosing the right gear and maintaining awareness gives your puppy the freedom to explore safely. With these practices in place, you can confidently move forward, knowing your puppy is well-equipped for their outdoor adventures.

Chapter 9

Busy Owners 10-Minute Training Strategies

Aconsistent 10-minute daily training plan is designed to fit seamlessly into your busy life while ensuring your puppy develops essential skills. Energy and focus come in short bursts with puppies, they get tired quickly and nap often. Focusing on short, engaging sessions can ensure you have your puppies complete focus and can really help with your busy schedule.

Training sessions don't need to be extended to be impactful. Short, focused sessions are often more effective for puppies whose attention spans rival a toddler's. A study from Preventive Vet suggests that 3 to 4 minutes per skill is ideal, preventing fatigue and maintaining interest. Concentrating on brief intervals allows your puppy to absorb commands without becoming overwhelmed. Divide your 10-minute session into segments of 2–3 minutes, each focusing on a different command. This approach not only reinforces skills but also keeps training fun. Prioritize commands that address your puppy's current needs, whether it's sitting politely or mastering the "stay" command. This method ensures that each session is tailored to your puppy's growth, promoting steady progress.

Selecting the right exercises for daily practice requires a balance between essential skills and engaging activities. You can begin with basic obedience commands, like "sit," "stay," or "come," which are fundamental for a well-behaved dog. These commands lay the groundwork for more complex behaviors and are crucial for safety and communication. Weave in fun tricks or activities to maintain your puppy's interest and enthusiasm. Teaching your puppy to "shake hands" or "high five" entertains and strengthens the human-dog bond through interaction and positive reinforcement. Rotating these exercises keeps the training fresh and exciting, ensuring your puppy looks forward to each session with anticipation.

Variety is the spice of life, and it's no different in puppy training. Introducing new commands periodically challenges your puppy and prevents boredom. This variety stimulates your puppy's mind, enhancing their ability to adapt and learn. It also mitigates the risk of boredom, which can stall progress and diminish engagement. As your puppy masters each new skill, their confidence grows, paving the way for more advanced training. By keeping the sessions lively and varied, you cultivate a learning environment that is both enjoyable and effective, fostering a lifelong love for learning in your puppy.

To bring these concepts to life, consider a sample daily training plan. Begin with a simple warm-up command like "sit," which your puppy likely knows well. Use this as an opportunity to build confidence and set a positive tone for the session. As your puppy successfully completes the command, offer praise and a treat, reinforcing the behavior. Progress to a more challenging skill, such as the "stay" command, requiring focus and patience. This not only tests your puppy's ability to maintain composure but also enhances their impulse control. Conclude the session with a well-mastered trick, like "shake hands," ending on a high note that leaves your puppy feeling accomplished and eager for the next session.

Reflection Section: Training Progress

Take a moment to journal your puppy's training progress. Document which commands they respond to best and any areas needing improvement. Reflect on how these short sessions fit into your daily routine. Reflect on the duration for which your puppy can maintain the "stay" command or identify new commands to introduce based on your puppy's interests and strengths. This reflection allows you to tailor future sessions, ensuring they remain challenging and rewarding. Regularly reviewing your puppy's progress ensures that you stay attuned to their developmental needs, guiding them effectively through each growth stage.

Blending Training into Everyday Activities

By integrating training into your daily routines, you capitalize on these opportunities, making efficient use of time while reinforcing good behavior. During meal preparation, for instance, practice basic commands like "sit" or "stay." While you're chopping vegetables or stirring a pot, take a moment to ask your puppy to sit quietly beside you. Reward their compliance with a small treat or kind word, and soon, they'll associate the kitchen hustle with calmness and obedience. This method reinforces training and teaches your puppy patience, helping them learn that they don't need to be the center of attention in every scenario.

Daily routines are filled with opportunities to reinforce training. When you're about to open a door or gate, whether heading outside for a walk or moving between rooms, pause and ask your puppy to sit before proceeding. This simple act teaches impulse control and respect for boundaries, making transitions smoother. Similarly, household chores present unexpected training moments. If your puppy gets curious while you're folding laundry or dusting, use the "leave it" command to redirect their attention away from the distractions. These everyday interactions are perfect for reinforcing commands, helping your puppy understand that obedience isn't just for dedicated training sessions but is part of how you interact throughout the day.

Life's unpredictability often presents training moments, and it's important to seize these opportunities for reinforcement. Picture unexpected visitors arriving at your doorstep. Instead of letting your puppy's excitement take over, reward their calm behavior with a treat or praise. This positive reinforcement encourages good manners and teaches your puppy to handle surprises gracefully. Another scenario might involve practicing the "stay" command while you unload groceries. As bags pile up at your feet, ask your puppy to remain still nearby, slowly extending their stay as you move items inside. These moments are invaluable, teaching your puppy to focus and follow instructions in real-world situations.

The atmosphere in which you train your puppy plays a big role in their success. Maintaining a positive, encouraging environment during these impromptu sessions is key. Use an upbeat tone and generous praise to show your puppy that training is fun and rewarding. This approach keeps your puppy engaged and eager to learn, even during mundane tasks. Keeping these training interactions brief prevents fatigue and ensures your puppy remains attentive and responsive. The goal is to weave training seamlessly into your life, making it a natural extension of how you communicate and bond with your puppy.

Maintaining Consistency Amidst a Busy Schedule

Life often feels like an intricate dance, with work, family, and personal commitments pulling you in different directions. This can make maintaining a consistent training routine challenging. You may find that unpredictable work schedules throw a wrench into your planned activities. One day, you're home early, and the next, you rush to meet deadlines late into the evening. Travel commitments add another layer of complexity, taking you away from home and disrupting your puppy's routine. Even household changes, such as the arrival of a new family member or a pet, can shift the dynamics and make it harder to stick to a training schedule. Recognizing these obstacles is the first step in addressing them.

Overcoming time constraints in such a hectic environment calls for practical solutions. Technology can be your ally here; setting phone reminders or alarms for scheduled training sessions can help ensure you don't overlook these crucial moments amidst your busy day. This simple tool keeps the idea of training front and center, prompting you to take those few minutes to engage with your puppy. Short breaks during the day can also serve as quick practice sessions. Maybe it's a five-minute break between work calls, while on lunch break, or even a pause while dinner simmers. These brief interactions reinforce training without demanding large chunks of your time, making them manageable even on the busiest days.

Creating a flexible training schedule can accommodate the ebb and flow of daily life. Instead of rigid daily tasks, plan weekly goals that allow you to adjust as needed. This approach allows you to adapt to unexpected changes without derailing your puppy's learning. If certain days are busier, consider batch training on less hectic days to make up for missed sessions. This adaptability ensures that training remains consistent, even when your schedule doesn't. By prioritizing flexibility, you maintain momentum while accommodating life's unpredictability's.

Involving family members in the training process can significantly enhance consistency. Sharing responsibilities not only lightens your load, but also ensures your puppy receives consistent cues from everyone involved. Assign specific commands to different family members, making training a collective effort. This division of labor ensures that each person can focus on mastering a particular skill with the puppy, providing continuity and reinforcement. As previously mentioned, creating the journal serves as an ideal method for monitoring progress, providing an invaluable resource for all family members to stay updated on the puppy's achievements and areas needing improvement. This allows everyone to note successes, challenges, and strategies, ensuring that the entire household is aligned in their approach. It's a collaborative tool that keeps everyone informed and engaged, strengthening the team effort in raising a well-trained puppy.

Tracking Progress and Celebrating Milestones

In the busyness of training a puppy, it's easy to overlook the subtle yet significant progress made each day. Documenting these achievements can be a powerful motivator for you and your puppy. Imagine the satisfaction of looking back at a journal of commands mastered and new skills introduced. This record is a testament to the hard work and dedication you've both invested. Whether it's the triumphant moment when your puppy finally stays on command, or the first time they successfully navigate a new trick, each entry in your journal captures a milestone in their development. Noting these behavioral improvements or breakthroughs provides a sense of accomplishment and highlights areas where your puppy excels, offering insight into their unique strengths and potential.

Keeping track of progress requires the right tools and techniques. In today's digital age, apps or spreadsheets can be invaluable in charting daily accomplishments. These platforms allow you to log each training session, track the duration and success of different commands, and even set reminders for future goals. Additionally, taking videos to record development over time visually offers a dynamic way to see how far your puppy has come. These clips can reveal subtle changes in posture, confidence, and responsiveness that might go unnoticed. By comparing videos from different stages of training, you can celebrate the progress made and identify any areas that need further attention.

Celebrating small victories is crucial in maintaining motivation and building confidence. Each new trick or command mastered is a triumph deserving of recognition. Organizing mini-celebrations, perhaps with a special treat or a favorite game, reinforces the positive experience of learning. These celebrations provide a reward for your puppy and a reminder of the joy that comes with each new achievement. Consider treating your puppy to a special outing, like a trip to the park or a play date with a fellow furry friend. Alternatively, a new toy can serve as a tangible symbol of their success, offering entertainment and encouragement.

Setting realistic training goals is essential in maintaining momentum and avoiding frustration. Establish achievable milestones for each week or month, ensuring they align with your puppy's learning pace. Short-term goals provide a clear focus, making it easier to track progress and adapt as needed. Adjust these goals as your puppy grows and develops to reflect their evolving abilities and interests. This flexibility allows you to tailor training to their individual needs, fostering a sense of accomplishment and encouraging continued growth.

By integrating these practices into your training routine, you create a structured environment supporting your puppy's development and your own sense of achievement. Tracking progress and celebrating milestones enhances the training experience and strengthens the bond between you and your puppy. This section has illustrated that dedicating just 10 minutes a day to your pup's training can be profoundly effective, laying a solid foundation for the exciting next steps in your shared journey.

Chapter 10

Positive Reinforcement Strategies

Imagine when your puppy first sits on cue, those big eyes looking up at you, tail wagging in anticipation. It's more than just a cute trick—it's the embodiment of the powerful connection between stimulus and response that lies at the heart of positive reinforcement. This section delves into the science behind this approach, exploring why it works and how you can harness it to shape your puppy's behavior. At its core, positive reinforcement relies on the principle that behaviors followed by rewards are more likely to be repeated. This simple concept is grounded in the broader framework of effective conditioning, where dogs learn to associate their actions with consequences. By adding something enjoyable, like a treat or praise, you increase the frequency of a desired behavior. This creates a powerful loop of learning that encourages your puppy to seek out and repeat positive actions.

The connection between stimulus and response is intricately tied to developing neural pathways in the brain. Each time your puppy receives a reward for a specific behavior, it strengthens the neural connections associated with that action. Over time, these pathways become more robust, making the behavior more automatic and ingrained. The impact of positive reinforcement extends beyond merely teaching commands; it fosters a mindset of eager participation and willingness to learn.

Timing plays a pivotal role in the effectiveness of positive reinforcement. Rewards need to be delivered immediately following the desired behavior. This timing is crucial because it bridges the gap between the action and the consequence, ensuring that your puppy makes a clear association. The critical window for associating an action with a reward is often just a few seconds. Any delay can weaken the connection, making it harder for your puppy to understand which behavior earned the reward. Quick, consistent reinforcement helps your puppy draw a direct line between their actions and the positive outcome, accelerating the learning process and fostering a sense of accomplishment.

The success of positive reinforcement is supported by a wealth of research, illustrating its superiority over training methods that rely on punishment or negative reinforcement. Studies have consistently demonstrated that dogs trained with positive reinforcement exhibit fewer behavioral issues and develop a deeper bond with their caregivers. The long-term benefits are clear: enhanced obedience, heightened confidence, and reduced stress levels among dogs. This compassionate training approach does more than teach your dog the right behaviors; it fosters an environment where they feel secure, appreciated, and motivated to excel. Your puppy's visible joy and eagerness during training sessions are powerful evidence of the method's effectiveness.

Positive reinforcement is well-documented in numerous studies, highlighting its benefits over other training methods. For instance, research comparing positive reinforcement with aversive techniques, such as physical corrections or reprimands, consistently shows that dogs trained with positive methods exhibit fewer behavioral problems and a stronger bond with their owners. Long-term outcomes of positive reinforcement include improved obedience, increased confidence, and reduced stress in dogs. This humane approach teaches your puppy what to do and creates an environment where they feel safe, valued, and motivated to succeed. The joy and enthusiasm you see in your puppy during training sessions are testaments to the effectiveness of this approach.

Despite its proven benefits, positive reinforcement is sometimes misunderstood. A common misconception is that it equates to bribery, implying that dogs are only behaving for treats. In reality, positive reinforcement is about reinforcing good behavior, not coaxing it with rewards. Over time, as behaviors become ingrained, the frequency of rewards can be reduced, shifting to praise or affection as primary motivators. Another concern is the fear of creating dependency on rewards. However, when managed correctly, positive reinforcement encourages natural motivation, where the act of performing the behavior becomes rewarding in itself. This transition from external to internal motivation is a hallmark of successful, positive reinforcement training, enabling your puppy to thrive in a nurturing and supportive environment.

Reflection Section: Understanding Positive Reinforcement

Take a moment to consider how you can apply the principles of positive reinforcement in your daily interactions with your puppy. Reflect on recent training sessions and identify moments where immediate rewards could have strengthened learning. Consider how you might adjust your timing to enhance the effectiveness of your training. Journaling these experiences can provide valuable insights into your puppy's responsiveness and help you refine your approach. By embracing the principles outlined in this section, you're not just training a puppy—you're fostering a lifelong partnership built on trust, respect, and mutual understanding.

Choosing the Best Rewards for Your Puppy

Identifying what motivates your puppy can feel like unlocking a treasure chest of possibilities. Each puppy is unique, with its own preferences and quirks, and discovering what makes your puppy tick is a rewarding part of the training process. Experiment with different treats to see which lights up your puppy's eyes. You might notice that pieces of chicken or lamb quickly become favorites with their rich flavors and enticing aromas. Cheese cubes or even small bits of hot dogs can also be irresistible. A dog trainer once told me hot dogs were like ice cream to dogs-who doesn't like ice cream! Pay attention to how your puppy reacts to each option. Does their tail wag more enthusiastically for one treat over another? Observing these reactions helps you pinpoint which treats hold the most value for your puppy, increasing their willingness to engage in training.

But treats aren't the only motivators. Toys can be equally effective, especially for puppies with a playful streak. Introduce various toys to see which ones capture your puppy's interest. Some puppies might go wild for a squeaky toy, while others might prefer a tug rope or a ball. Notice how your puppy engages with each toy, and use this information to your advantage. Incorporating their favorite toy into training sessions can make learning feel like a game, keeping your puppy excited and eager to participate. Similarly, don't underestimate the power of affection. Some puppies are deeply motivated by praise and gentle petting. If your puppy thrives on attention, offering a few moments of undivided love can be just as rewarding as a tasty treat.

Maintaining your puppy's motivation requires a touch of creativity and variety. Just as humans tire of the same meal daily, puppies can become bored with repetitive rewards. Keep things fresh by rotating treats and toys, ensuring your puppy remains engaged and interested. This variety prevents training from becoming monotonous, sustaining your puppy's enthusiasm. You might use high-value treats like beef jerky for challenging tasks and switch to a different reward for more routine exercises. Similarly, alternate between toys and treats to keep your puppy guessing. This unpredictability heightens their curiosity and encourages them to stay focused, wondering what delightful reward will come next.

When selecting rewards, consider their nutritional value and size. Treats used in training should be small enough to avoid overfeeding but flavorful enough to capture your puppy's attention. Opt for treats that are nutritious and made from quality ingredients. This ensures that training remains a healthy endeavor for your puppy. Additionally, think about the safety and suitability of toys. Choose toys matching your puppy's age and size to prevent choking hazards. Durable toys that withstand teething and rough play are ideal, ensuring they last through many training sessions. You create a rewarding experience that benefits you and your puppy by prioritizing safety and quality.

Customizing rewards to suit your puppy's individual preferences can transform training from a task into a joy. For energetic puppies, incorporating playtime as a reward can channel their energy positively. After successfully following a command, reward them with a quick game of fetch or a playful tug session. This reinforces the behavior and provides an outlet for their boundless energy. On the other hand, for puppies who are more reserved or anxious, verbal praise and gentle petting may be more effective. Offering a soothing touch or a kind word can reassure them, reinforcing their confidence and trust in you. Tailoring rewards in this way acknowledges your puppy's personality, making training a more personalized and enjoyable experience.

Reinforcing Good Behavior in Real-Time

Catching the exact moment your puppy calmly greets a new friend, tail wagging gently, eyes bright. This is the perfect opportunity to reinforce good behavior; timing is everything. Linking it to a reward within seconds is crucial when your puppy performs a desirable action. This swift connection helps your puppy understand which behavior earned the praise or treat. Think of it as snapping a photo at just the right moment. If you wait too long, the moment is lost, and your puppy might not associate the reward with the action you want to encourage. This precise timing ensures that your puppy knows exactly what behavior to repeat in the future.

Capturing these moments as they happen requires tools and techniques you can rely on instantly. One effective method is using a clicker. This small device emits a distinct sound when your puppy does something you want to encourage. The clicker acts as a marker, signaling to your puppy that a reward is coming. Its effectiveness lies in cutting through distractions, providing a clear cue that your puppy understands. Alongside the clicker, quick verbal cues are also powerful. Simple words like "Yes!" or "Good!" can work wonders, especially when used in the same enthusiastic tone each time. These verbal affirmations signal that your puppy has done well, encouraging them to repeat the behavior.

Marking desired behaviors offers clarity in training, distinguishing between different actions your puppy might perform. For instance, marking a calm sit with a click or verbal cue helps your puppy differentiate it from other behaviors like jumping or barking. This differentiation is vital in helping your puppy understand what you want from them. By consistently marking and rewarding your desired behaviors, you set clear expectations, reducing confusion and reinforcing learning. This clarity makes training more efficient and enjoyable for you and your puppy, fostering a positive environment where your puppy feels secure and eager to learn.

The beauty of positive reinforcement lies in its seamless integration into everyday life. Training doesn't have to be confined to scheduled sessions. Every interaction with your puppy is an opportunity to reinforce good habits. Rewarding calmness when your puppy meets a new person helps them learn that polite greetings lead to positive outcomes. Similarly, reinforcing patience during grooming or handling teaches your puppy that remaining still and cooperative is beneficial. These small, everyday moments add up, gradually shaping your puppy's behavior and building trust and understanding. By embedding reinforcement into daily interactions, you transform ordinary encounters into meaningful learning experiences.

Incorporating these strategies into your routine requires consistency and attentiveness. It's about being present in the moment, ready to reward your puppy as they navigate their world. Whether you're out for a walk or relaxing at home, be prepared to recognize and encourage the behaviors you want to see more of. This attentiveness strengthens your puppy's learning and deepens your connection, reinforcing your role as a source of guidance and support. Over time, you'll find that your puppy eagerly looks to you for cues, confident in their ability to please you, and secure in knowing their efforts are met with love and appreciation.

Adjusting Techniques for Different Temperaments

When training your puppy, adopting a one-size-fits-all approach can be ineffective, especially when each puppy comes with unique personality traits. Just like people, puppies have individual temperaments that influence their response to training methods. Recognizing these differences is crucial in crafting a training approach that resonates with your puppy. Some puppies are naturally shy, displaying signs of stress or discomfort in new situations. You might notice them cowering, avoiding eye contact, or hesitating to explore. For these sensitive souls, a quieter, more relaxed training method can help build their confidence. Using a soft voice and slow movements minimizes stress and encourages them to engage without feeling overwhelmed.

On the other hand, some puppies are more assertive, brimming with energy and curiosity. These little explorers thrive on active, energetic training sessions that match their zest for life. Incorporating play and movement into their training keeps them engaged and channels their energy positively. Activities like fetch or agility exercises can be integrated into learning commands, making the process feel like a game. This approach caters to their lively nature and helps burn off excess energy, leading to a more focused and content puppy. Balancing the intensity of these sessions with moments of calm ensures that your puppy remains attentive and ready to learn.

Continuous observation plays a pivotal role in refining your training methods. By closely watching your puppy's reactions to different rewards and techniques, you gain valuable insights into what works best for them. Maybe your puppy lights up at the sight of a specific toy or shows more enthusiasm when training happens outdoors. Noting these preferences allows you to tailor your approach, maximizing engagement and effectiveness. This attentive observation is important when introducing new commands or routines. If you notice signs of reluctance or resistance, it might be time to adjust your strategy. Perhaps the training environment is too distracting, or the rewards aren't motivating enough. By being flexible and responsive, you ensure that training remains a positive experience for your puppy.

Handling resistance is another aspect of training that requires patience and creativity. Some puppies may be hesitant when faced with unfamiliar tasks, showing reluctance through avoidance or distraction. Introducing new techniques can help build their confidence. Start with small steps, rewarding each successful attempt, no matter how minor. This incremental approach reduces pressure and fosters a sense of achievement. If a particular behavior or command continues to pose challenges, seeking professional advice might be beneficial. A dog trainer can offer fresh perspectives and personalized strategies to overcome specific hurdles, ensuring your puppy receives the support they need to thrive.

Ultimately, the key to successful training lies in adaptability and understanding. Acknowledging and responding to your puppy's temperament creates an environment where they feel safe and motivated to learn. This strengthens your bond and lays the foundation for a relationship built on trust and mutual respect. As you navigate the training journey, remember that it's a collaborative effort where you and your puppy learn and grow together. Each small victory is a testament to your dedication and your puppy's potential, paving the way for a lifetime of shared adventures.

Chapter 11

Managing Common Behavioral Issues

The sun dips below the horizon, casting a warm glow over your living room as you settle in for the evening. Your puppy, however, seems oblivious to the day's end, bursting with hyper activity, jumping on you, hopping around while barking at every passing shadow and pounces on your slipper in a sneak attack and begins chewing it to bits. This scene, familiar to many puppy owners, underscores the challenge of managing behavioral issues. These behaviors can test your patience and disrupt the tranquility of home life.

Let's take a look at these issues individually. Understanding the triggers behind your puppy's barking is the first step in addressing this common issue. Puppies bark for various reasons, from unfamiliar noises outside to sheer boredom or the simple desire for your attention. Identifying these triggers requires keen observation and situational analysis, piecing together clues from the environment and your puppy's behavior to reveal the underlying stressors.

Once you've pinpointed why your puppy barks, you can begin to address the behavior through targeted training techniques. One effective method is to teach your puppy the "quiet" command. Start by allowing your puppy to bark a few times, then gently say "quiet" while holding a treat. As soon as they stop barking, reward them immediately. This reinforces the connection between silence and positive outcomes. Over time, your puppy will learn that ceasing to bark when commanded leads to rewards. Another useful technique is the "speak" command, which teaches your puppy to bark on cue. This might sound counterintuitive, but it gives you control over when your puppy barks. By establishing a command for barking, you can also signal when it's time to be quiet, providing a balanced approach to managing this vocal behavior.

Physical and mental stimulation play crucial roles in mitigating excessive barking. A well-exercised puppy is less likely to bark out of boredom or pent-up energy. Incorporating daily walks and playtime into your routine helps burn off energy and strengthens the bond between you and your puppy. These activities provide mental stimulation, reducing the likelihood of boredom-induced barking. Introducing puzzle toys can further engage your puppy's mind, challenging them to solve problems and stay occupied. These toys tap into your puppy's natural curiosity and intelligence, offering a constructive outlet for their energy and reducing the impulse to bark at every little thing.

Creating a calm environment is another effective strategy for minimizing barking. External sounds like traffic or noisy neighbors can trigger barking fits. You can help mask these sounds with white noise machines, creating a soothing auditory backdrop that reduces your puppy's response to outside disturbances. Additionally, providing a safe retreat area offers your puppy a haven where they can escape overwhelming stimuli. This space, whether it's a comfy bed tucked in a quiet corner or a designated room, becomes a sanctuary of calmness. It's important to ensure this area remains consistent and inviting, reinforcing its role as a peaceful retreat whenever your puppy feels anxious or overstimulated.

Reflection Section: Identifying Bark Triggers

Take a moment to reflect on your puppy's barking patterns. Consider adding a section to your journal where you note the times and situations in which your puppy barks. What are the common triggers? Is it the mail carrier's arrival, a neighbor's dog, or perhaps a specific time of day? Use this information to adjust your approach; planning walks or playtime around potential triggers to preemptively reduce barking episodes. This proactive strategy helps manage barking and deepens your understanding of your puppy's needs and preferences, fostering a harmonious household environment.

Redirecting Destructive Chewing

Puppies see the world through their mouths, and chewing is a big part of that exploration. It's not just an innocent pastime; it's a vital part of their development. Imagine your puppy's mouth as their primary tool for understanding the environment, much like how infants use their hands. Teething, which usually kicks in around four months, propels this behavior as your puppy seeks relief from sore gums. The discomfort drives them to gnaw on anything within reach, from shoes to furniture legs. Boredom makes this worse, leading to destructive habits as they seek stimulation in their surroundings. The urge to chew is natural, but without guidance, it can lead to a household in disarray.

Finding the right chew toys can make all the difference. Durable rubber toys are perfect for teething relief, offering a satisfying texture that massages sore gums without the risk of breaking teeth. Look for options that can be frozen, as the cold can soothe inflamed gums. Treat-dispensing toys are another excellent choice, engaging your puppy's mind while keeping them occupied. These toys provide a dual benefit: they satisfy the urge to chew and offer a mental challenge that prevents boredom. When selecting toys, prioritize those labeled specifically for puppies, ensuring they're safe and appropriately sized in order to avoid choking hazards. The right toys protect your belongings and support your puppy's developmental needs.

Redirecting your puppy's chewing behavior requires patience and consistency. The "leave it" command is invaluable here, teaching your puppy to step away from inappropriate items. Practice this command in low-stakes situations, gradually increasing the challenge as your puppy masters it. When your puppy is caught chewing something they shouldn't, calmly use the command and swap the item with an appropriate toy. This reinforces the idea that while chewing is acceptable, some items are off-limits. Consistency is key; the more you reinforce this behavior, the sooner your puppy will understand the boundaries. Praise and rewards for choosing the right toy reinforce positive behavior, encouraging them to make good choices independently.

Supervision remains crucial in preventing destructive chewing. Puppies are curious creatures, and without guidance, they can quickly find themselves in trouble. Keeping valuable items out of reach is a straightforward way to mitigate risk. Store shoes, clothing, and other tempting objects in closed closets or high shelves, removing the temptation altogether. Supervised play sessions offer additional opportunities to reinforce appropriate chewing behavior, allowing you to step in and redirect as needed. These sessions also provide a chance to bond with your puppy, building trust and understanding through shared activities. Puppy-proofing your home isn't just about protecting your belongings; it's about creating a safe space for your puppy to explore and grow without unnecessary restrictions.

In the quest to manage chewing, remember that your puppy is learning and adapting at every turn. They're driven by curiosity and instinct, exploring a world that's new and exciting. Providing appropriate outlets for their energy and instincts supports their growth while maintaining harmony in your home. As you guide your puppy through this stage, you'll find that the effort you invest in training and supervision pays off in a well-adjusted, confident dog who understands their place in your household.

Teaching Your Puppy Not to Bite

Puppies explore the world with their mouths—it's how they play, interact, and even show affection. Nibbling on hands may seem harmless at first, even cute. But if not gently redirected early on, this behavior can develop into hard mouthing or biting as your puppy grows. That's why it's important to set clear, kind boundaries from the start.

There could be several reasons behind your puppy biting. *Teething Discomfort*: The experience of teething can cause discomfort, leading puppies to chew on whatever they can find, including human fingers. *Learning Through Play*: In the absence of littermates, puppies look to their human family to learn bite inhibition, a lesson they would typically acquire through play with their siblings. *Seeking Interaction*: Puppies may also bite as a way to engage or attract attention, interpreting even negative responses like pulling away as encouragement for their behavior.

Try to avoid using negative reactions such as yelling, smacking, or forcibly closing your puppy's mouth. These actions can lead to confusion or fear and typically make the unwanted behavior worse. Focus instead on guiding your puppy towards desired actions, highlighting positive behaviors rather than just correcting the undesirable ones.

Ways to avoid this becoming a bad habit. When your puppy begins to mouth your hands, quickly redirect their attention with a chew toy. As they shift their focus and bite the toy, shower them with praise for choosing the appropriate item to chew on. *Say*: "Good chew!" in a happy voice.

It's a good idea to keep a soft plush toy or teething ring handy at all times during the early weeks.

Implement a Gentle, Recognizable Signal if your puppy applies too much pressure with their bite, emit a gentle, high-pitched "ouch!" and pause any ongoing play immediately. This approach simulates the reaction they would receive from a playmate, teaching them the limits of acceptable play. Afterward, allow for a short break (5–10 seconds) to underline the message that biting disrupts the fun. Consistency is key. Ensuring that all household members respond in this uniform manner helps your puppy understand and adhere to these boundaries more quickly.

Reinforce Gentle Behavior. Capitalize on moments when your puppy displays behaviors like licking, sitting calmly, or gentle mouthing by immediately rewarding them. These instances are perfect opportunities to encourage and reinforce self-control. Reward them with a treat or affectionate praise during moments of calm and soft interaction, and withhold rewards when they exhibit rough or mouthy behavior.

Should redirection and verbal cues prove ineffective, it's important to calmly conclude the play session. Either walk away or softly guide your puppy into a playpen equipped with a toy. This action clearly communicates that rough play results in the end of playtime.

Encouraging your puppy to understand the appropriate pressure for mouthing can be a gentle process. Allow for soft mouthing during playtime, but if their bite becomes too firm, clearly say "ouch" and momentarily stop the interaction. This will help your puppy gradually learn the acceptable strength of their bite through consistent feedback.

Consistency in training is essential, as it's important for all family members and visitors to use the same methods and commands. Mixed signals can confuse your puppy and slow down their training progress.

When to Seek Professional Guidance: Should your puppy's biting advance to aggression, resource guarding, or cause injury, it's crucial to seek the expertise of a certified positive reinforcement trainer or a veterinary behaviorist in your area. These behaviors could require tailored guidance and methods that extend beyond basic training recommendations.

Tackling Jumping Up on People

Arriving home after a long day, you're greeted by your puppy's enthusiastic leaps. While endearing, this jumping behavior can quickly become problematic, especially when your puppy matures into a larger dog. So, why do puppies jump? At its core, jumping is a form of seeking attention. Puppies instinctively crave interaction and often jump up to be nearer. They perceive the world from a lower vantage point, where your hands, eyes, and mouth are all above them, viewed as symbols of connection and positive engagement. It's also a behavior rooted in excitement. Your return home or the arrival of a guest sparks joy, and jumping is their way of expressing it. However, puppies can misinterpret this as a proper greeting, not realizing it might be overwhelming or even hazardous for the person on the receiving end.

To manage jumping, it's crucial to redirect this behavior to something more appropriate right from the beginning. Teaching the "off" command is a valuable tool in your training arsenal. Begin by calmly stepping back when your puppy jumps, avoiding eye contact or petting. Firmly say "off" and wait for all four paws to return to the ground. Once they comply, immediately reward them with praise or a treat. This positive reinforcement helps them associate the command with the desired action. Another effective method is to encourage sitting during greetings. As your puppy approaches, ask them to sit before they have a chance to jump. Reward them promptly when they do, reinforcing that sitting is the behavior that earns them attention and affection.

Consistency in responses is key to curbing jumping. Puppies learn through repetition, and mixed signals can confuse them. Ensure that everyone interacting with your puppy follows the same protocol. If your puppy jumps on someone, instruct them to turn away and ignore the behavior. This lack of acknowledgment removes the reward of attention that jumping seeks. Once your puppy calms down and has all four paws on the floor, encourage everyone to lavish them with attention and treats. This uniform response teaches your puppy that calm behavior is the only way to receive the interaction they crave. Consistency helps your puppy learn quickly, making it easier to adopt the new behavior.

Alternative greeting rituals can transform how your puppy interacts with people. Encourage your puppy to fetch a toy when guests arrive. This distracts them from jumping and provides a positive outlet for their excitement. Practice these interactions by keeping a favorite toy near the door. When someone arrives, guide your puppy to retrieve it, offering praise and rewards when they comply.

Additionally, practicing calm, seated greetings with family members can reinforce this behavior. Have family members approach your seated puppy calmly, rewarding them for staying down. This practice helps your puppy associate calmness with greetings, reducing their impulse to jump in excitement.

By focusing on these techniques, you can guide your puppy to develop polite greeting habits that will serve them well throughout their life. The effort invested in training today leads to a more harmonious experience for you and your puppy, fostering an environment where both canine and human can interact comfortably and safely.

Strategies for Calming Hyperactivity

Hyperactivity in puppies often manifests as a whirlwind of energy, with your puppy bouncing off the walls, unable to settle. Recognizing the signs and triggers is the first step towards managing it effectively. Hyperactivity frequently stems from a buildup of excessive energy due to insufficient exercise. Puppies require ample opportunities to expend their natural exuberance, and when these outlets are lacking, they may resort to hyperactive behavior as a release. Overstimulation from chaotic environments can also play a significant role. A bustling household with constant noise and activity might leave a puppy feeling overwhelmed, resulting in seemingly endless bouts of frenetic movement. Identifying these triggers is crucial to understanding and addressing the root causes of your puppy's hyperactive tendencies.

Once you've recognized the signs, redirect your puppy's energy through structured activities. Establishing regular play sessions with clear start and end times can create a sense of routine and balance. These sessions should be interactive and engaging, allowing your puppy to channel their energy into positive outlets. Incorporate games that challenge their mind and body, such as fetch or tug-of-war, fostering focus and control. Consider introducing agility training or setting up obstacle courses in your backyard for a more advanced approach. These activities provide physical exercise and stimulate your puppy's intellect, keeping them engaged and mentally satisfied. Creating a structured routine gives your puppy a predictable and constructive way to burn off excess energy, reducing the likelihood of hyperactive outbursts.

During episodes of hyperactivity, calming techniques can help soothe your puppy and restore tranquility. Practicing deep breathing exercises with your puppy might sound unconventional, but it involves more than you might think. Sit calmly with your puppy, taking slow, deep breaths while gently petting them. Your calm presence and rhythmic breathing can help lower their energy levels, encouraging them to mirror your relaxed demeanor. Additionally, consider using calming aids like pressure wraps or pheromone diffusers. Pressure wraps apply gentle, constant pressure, similar to a comforting hug, which can help alleviate anxiety and calm an overstimulated puppy. Pheromone diffusers release synthetic versions of calming pheromones, creating a soothing environment that can help your puppy relax. These tools can be particularly effective during heightened excitement, providing reassurance and comfort.

A balanced daily routine is important for managing your puppy's energy levels. Establishing regular meals, play, and rest schedules creates a sense of predictability that can have a calming effect on your puppy. Consistent meal times help regulate energy levels, while scheduled play sessions ensure that your puppy receives the exercise they need. Equally important is integrating quiet time or nap breaks throughout the day. Much like human infants, puppies require ample sleep to support their growth and development. Providing designated times for rest prevents exhaustion and teaches your puppy the importance of downtime. These breaks offer an opportunity to recharge, reducing the likelihood of hyperactivity driven by fatigue. By maintaining a well-rounded routine, you create a harmonious environment where your puppy can thrive physically and emotionally.

As we bring this section to a close, remember that managing hyperactivity is an ongoing process that requires patience and consistency. By understanding the underlying causes and implementing structured routines, you pave the way for a well-adjusted companion. This journey, while challenging, is an integral part of fostering a strong bond with your puppy. As you continue to guide your puppy through these formative stages, you'll find that the strategies you've learned here will serve as a foundation for future sections.

Chapter 12

Fostering a Lifelong Bond

I magine stepping outside on a crisp morning, your puppy by your side, ears perked, and eyes bright with curiosity. You've both come a long way since the day you first brought them home, but the journey of understanding and connection continues. The bond between you and your puppy is built on communication, and much of this communication is non-verbal. With their boundless energy and expressive faces, puppies communicate a wealth of information through their body language. Understanding these subtle cues can unlock a deeper connection, transforming your relationship into profound trust and mutual understanding.

Understanding your puppy's body language is like learning a new language of movements and gestures that speak volumes about their feelings and needs. When a puppy licks their lips or yawns, these actions might seem insignificant, but they can indicate stress or anxiety, signaling that they need reassurance or a break from a stimulating environment. A wagging tail, often associated with happiness, can communicate different emotions depending on its position and speed. A slow wag might indicate uncertainty, while a fast wag usually signals excitement or eagerness. Recognizing these signs lets you respond thoughtfully to your puppy's emotional state, helping them feel secure and understood.

Ear positions are another vital component of a puppy's body language repertoire. Erect ears often signal alertness, suggesting your puppy is paying close attention to their surroundings. Conversely, ears flattened against the head can indicate fear or submission, a sign that your puppy might feel overwhelmed or intimidated. Observing these mood indicators provides valuable insight into your puppy's emotional world, allowing you to tailor your interactions and environment to suit their needs. A relaxed posture, with a partially open mouth and a lolling tongue, typically signals a content and comfortable puppy, inviting you to engage in gentle play or a quiet cuddle.

One of the most delightful body language cues is the play bow, where your puppy lowers their front legs while keeping their rear end in the air. This unmistakable gesture is an invitation to play, reflecting excitement and a desire for interaction. Responding to a play bow with a game or a toy acknowledges your puppy's request and strengthens the bond of companionship. By engaging in play when invited, you build a relationship of trust, where your puppy feels confident that you understand and respect their needs.

Observing your puppy's body language affects practical training and behavior management. By identifying cues that precede unwanted behaviors, such as restlessness or stiffness, you can anticipate and redirect these behaviors before they escalate. For instance, if you notice your puppy becoming tense around other dogs, you might choose to distract them with a toy or treat, guiding their focus away from potential conflict. This proactive approach minimizes stress and fosters a sense of security, reinforcing your role as a reliable and attentive partner.

Building trust through consistent responses to your puppy's body language is crucial for a harmonious relationship. When you acknowledge calming signals like a yawn or a shake-off with soothing words or actions, you communicate that you recognize their discomfort and are there to support them. This consistent acknowledgment helps your puppy learn that their feelings are valid and that they can rely on you for comfort and guidance. Over time, this mutual understanding cultivates a deep sense of trust, creating a foundation for a lifelong bond of love and companionship.

Reflection Section: Your Puppy's Language

Take a moment to reflect on your interactions with your puppy. Have you noticed any specific cues that indicate their mood or needs? Jot down a few observations in your journal, noting the situations in which these cues appear. This practice sharpens your skills in interpreting your puppy's body language. It enhances your ability to respond appropriately, fostering a more substantial connection built on empathy and understanding.

Playtime for Mental and Physical Stimulation

Shared playtime does more than expend energy; it strengthens the bond between you and your puppy. Through games like fetch, you learn to communicate without words, building a connection that relies on mutual enjoyment and trust. Fetch is more than a simple game—it's an opportunity for your puppy to learn to focus, follow commands, and return to you, reinforcing their understanding of your partnership. It's a dance of give and take, where each throw and return builds a little more trust and understanding of each other's rhythms and cues.

Interactive games that encourage owner-puppy interaction are vital. Whether it's a game of hide-and-seek where your puppy learns to use their nose to find you or a playful tug-of-war with a favorite rope, these activities strengthen your relationship. They teach your puppy to look to you for guidance and fun, reinforcing your role as a leader and companion. Toys that require your involvement, such as dispensing treats when manipulated correctly, are excellent tools for engaging your puppy's mind. These toys challenge your puppy to think, using their instincts to solve problems. This mental stimulation is as crucial as physical exercise, keeping your puppy sharp and eager to learn.

Incorporating varied play routines is essential to prevent boredom. A puppy needs stimulation, both mental and physical, to thrive. Rotating toys can maintain interest, ensuring that playtime remains fresh and exciting. Introducing new games or variations of old favorites keeps your puppy engaged and eager to see what fun awaits them next. Perhaps today, it's a puzzle toy filled with their favorite treats, and tomorrow, it's a basic scent game, hiding treats around the house for them to find. These activities challenge their mind, encouraging them to think and explore, fostering a sense of curiosity and adventure.

Supervision is key, especially when your puppy plays with other dogs. Even the most benign play can sometimes become too rough, so it's important to be nearby to intervene if necessary. Observing your puppy during these interactions keeps them safe and provides insight into their social behaviors, helping you guide them in learning appropriate play manners.

Playtime is not merely a means of burning energy. It's an opportunity for growth, learning, and bonding. Each game you play together is a thread that weaves the fabric of your relationship, creating a tapestry of shared experiences and mutual understanding. Through these playful interactions, you teach your puppy to trust you and see you as a provider and partner in fun and exploration. These moments spent in play are the building blocks of a lifelong bond, a stronger connection with each joyful romp and wag of the tail.

Building Confidence Through New Experiences

New environments are more than just a change of scenery —they are gateways to a world of confidence and adaptability. Each fresh experience shapes a well-rounded temperament and is crucial for your puppy's growth. Whether it's the rustle of leaves in a forest or the bustling energy of a city park, exposing your puppy to diverse settings enriches their understanding of the world. These experiences teach them to navigate different terrains, encounter new scents, and adapt to varied sounds, fostering resilience and curiosity.

Introducing your puppy to various social situations also plays a pivotal role in confidence-building. Interaction with diverse groups of people and animals provides invaluable lessons in social behavior and communication. Puppies learn to decode the non-verbal signals of other dogs and understand the gentle touch of a friendly hand. These interactions help them develop social skills, teaching them how to respond to different personalities and temperaments. By meeting new faces and wagging tails, they learn the nuances of social engagement, becoming more confident and at ease in varied company.

Ensuring these encounters are positive requires thoughtful planning. Start with low-stress situations, allowing your puppy to adjust at their own pace. Perhaps begin with a quiet afternoon at a friend's house, where your puppy can explore a new environment without feeling overwhelmed. Gradually increase the complexity of these experiences as they grow more comfortable. Pairing new experiences with high-value treats or praise makes a world of difference. A delicious reward for a brave step forward reinforces the behavior, encouraging your puppy to explore further and embrace the unknown. This positive reinforcement rewards bravery and cements the bond between you as your puppy learns to associate new adventures with your approval and support.

However, remaining attuned to your puppy's comfort levels is essential. Recognizing when they feel overwhelmed is key to preventing negative associations. Watch for signs like hesitancy or retreating behaviors, which may indicate your puppy needs a break. Adjusting the pace based on their responses shows their feelings are acknowledged and respected. Providing a retreat option, such as a quiet space or a comforting toy, offers your puppy a sense of safety when the world feels too big. This assurance bolsters their confidence, teaching them that it's okay to seek comfort and that new experiences can be approached at their own speed.

Incorporating positive reinforcement throughout these explorations is crucial. Rewarding your puppy for calm behavior and exploration reinforces their courage, encouraging them to venture further each time. This approach builds confidence and strengthens your relationship as your puppy learns you are a reliable source of support and encouragement. Over time, these experiences weave together to form a tapestry of confidence, resilience, and trust. Your puppy grows into an adult dog who meets the world head-on, eager to explore with you by their side.

Creating a Loving and Respectful Partnership

The heart of any strong relationship lies in mutual respect, which is no different when it comes to nurturing the bond between you and your puppy. Acknowledging your puppy's needs and boundaries is the cornerstone of this respect. It's about understanding when your puppy is tired and needs a nap or recognizing their need for space after a lively play session. Gentle handling and communication are key; these are not just about physical touches but also the tone of your voice and the patience in your actions. When you respect their boundaries, your puppy learns to trust you, knowing you will not push them beyond their limits. This mutual respect fosters a deeper bond, creating a safe space where your puppy feels valued and understood.

Trust and reliability build on this foundation of respect. Consistency in commands and routines is vital. When your puppy knows what to expect, they feel secure and confident in their environment. This is not just about feeding times or potty breaks but also how you interact with them daily. Providing a safe and predictable environment means setting up routines your puppy can rely on. Whether it's a morning walk or an evening cuddle, these habits reinforce their sense of security. By being consistent, you show your puppy that you are dependable, which is essential in building their trust. In turn, this trust makes them more responsive to training and more affectionate companions.

Techniques for nurturing a loving bond are varied, yet they all emphasize expressing affection and strengthening your connection. Daily rituals play a significant role here. Simple acts like grooming your puppy or setting aside time for cuddles reinforce your bond. These moments are about physical care and emotional connection, where your puppy feels your love and attention. Using positive reinforcement during these interactions further builds mutual respect. Rewarding good behavior with praise or treats shows your puppy that you value their efforts, encouraging them to continue engaging positively. This positive cycle strengthens your relationship, fostering a loving and respectful bond.

Maintaining this partnership requires a lifelong commitment. Your relationship with your puppy should be dynamic, evolving as they grow and learn. Continuing education and training throughout your puppy's life is crucial. It keeps both you and your puppy engaged and mentally stimulated. Training sessions can be opportunities for bonding, where learning becomes a shared experience. Engaging in activities that you and your puppy enjoy further solidifies your connection. Whether exploring a new hiking trail or visiting a new lake, shared interests deepen your relationship, making it richer and more fulfilling.

As you guide your puppy through the stages of life, remember that your role is not just as a caretaker but as a companion. Your commitment to understanding and respecting your puppy's needs, coupled with the consistency and love you provide, lays the groundwork for a partnership that will bring joy and fulfillment to both of you. This section closes the loop on building a relationship that thrives on mutual respect and trust, setting the stage for a harmonious life together. As we move forward, the focus shifts to practical applications and advanced training techniques to enhance the life you share with your puppy.

BONUS: 250 Puppy Names

Selecting the right name for your puppy is a thrilling step in your journey together! This section includes a curated list of over 250 dog names to inspire you in finding the ideal name for your new four-legged companion.

Funny Dog Names

Bark Twain	Biscuit	Boop	Bow Wow	Burrito	Butterball
Floof	Chewbarka	Chunky	Elmo	Furrball	Fuzz Lightyear
Giggles	Goofy	Hairy Pawter	Houndini	Jello	Jellybean
Jimmy Chew	Jumpy	Kevin	Meatball	Muttley	Nacho
Noodles	Captain	Nugget	Oreo	Ozzie	Pancake Paws
Peaches	Pecan	Pickles	Pudding	Quackers	Sausage
Scruffy	Sizzle	Snickers	Spud	Taco	Tater Tot
Uggs	Uncle Fuzz	Upsy Daisy	Waffles	Waggles	Waggy McTail
Wiggles	Woofgang	Wookie	Wick	Yappers	Yelp
Yeti	Yolo	Zoomie	Zippy	Zoodles	Zagnut

Popular Male Dog Names

Ace	Apollo	Archer	Axel	Bandit	Baxter	Beau
Benji	Benny	Blue	Boomer	Brody	Bruno	Buster
Charlie	Dexter	Diesel	Duke	Echo	Eli	Finn
Flash	Frank	George	Gus	Hank	Harley	Henry
Hudson	Hunter	Jack	Jackson	Jake	Jasper	Jax
Joey	Kobe	Koda	Leo	Loki	Louie	Max
Maverick	Melvin	Milo	Murphy	Nash	Nova	Odin
Oliver	Ollie	Onyx	Parker	Prince	Quincy	Ranger
Rex	Rocky	Roscoe	Rusty	Sam	Scout	Simba
Shadow	Snoop	Sparky	Tank	Teddy	Theo	Thor
Titan	Toby	Tucker	Tyson	Ulysses	Uno	Vader
Vinnie	Watson	Waylon	Wesley	Whiskey	Winston	Xander
Xavier	Yukon	Yogi	Yoda	Zain	Zech	Zeke
Zavier	Zeus	Ziggy	Zion	Zip	Zoomy	Zorro

Popular Female Dog Names

Abby	Angel	Annie	Aspen	Athena	Bailey	Bella
Biscuit	Bonnie	Cali	Callie	Charli	Chloe	Cinder
Cleo	Cleopatra	Coco	Cassie	Daisy	Dakota	Delilah
Diamond	Dixie	Dolly	Echo	Eden	Ella	Ellie
Ember	Faith	Faye	Fiona	Freya	Freida	Gabby
Georgia	Ginger	Grace	Gracie	Greta	Hannah	Harper
Hazel	Holly	Hope	Ivy	Jade	Jasmine	Josie
Joy	Juniper	Kessa	Kiki	Kona	Lady	Layla
Lexi	Lily	Lola	Lucy	Luna	Maggie	Maple
Marley	Maya	Mia	Millie	Minnie	Mischa	Missy
Molly	Mocha	Nala	Nova	Olive	Paisley	Pearl
Penelope	Penny	Phoebe	Piper	Poppy	Quinn	Quincy
Raven	Riley	Rosie	Roxie	Ruby	Sadie	Sasha
Scarlett	Scout	Sirka	Skye	Stella	Sugar	Sunny
Summer	Tessa	Thea	Tilly	Tink	Tinker	Tulip
Violet	Winnie	Wren	Xena	Yara	Yasmin	Yvette
Yvonne	Zara	Zelda	Zoey	Zola	Zozo	Zuri

Conclusion

These techniques can help with training your puppy, a young dog as well as senior dogs. As we come to the end of our journey together, I want to take a moment to reflect on the path we've traveled. This book was born from my family's decades of experience raising German Shepherds. It's a collection of the lessons learned, the joys shared, and the challenges overcome by our customers and us. Through these pages, I hope you've found a guide and a companion—

a resource you can return to as you navigate the rewarding adventure of raising your dream dog.

We have helped you prepare for your puppies' arrival and bring your new addition home. But, the six essential steps we've explored together are at the heart of this book. From potty training to mastering leash walking, each step builds upon the last, creating a solid foundation for a lifetime of love and companionship. We've delved into the importance of establishing routines, the power of positive reinforcement, and the art of socialization. These are the building blocks of a well-adjusted, confident puppy and the keys to forging an unbreakable bond between you and your furry friend.

I hope you've come to understand the significance of consistency, patience, and empathy in your training approach. Puppies, like children, thrive on structure and understanding. By learning your puppy's unique language, celebrating their successes, and gently guiding them through challenges, you create an environment where they feel safe, valued, and eager to learn. This is the essence of positive reinforcement—not just a training technique but a philosophy of love and respect.

One of the key messages I hope you take away from this book is that raising a puppy doesn't have to be an all-consuming task. The methods outlined here are designed with the busy owner in mind—practical, efficient, and easy to integrate into your daily life. Whether you're a first-time puppy parent or a seasoned pro, these techniques will help you make the most of every moment with your dog, turning everyday interactions into opportunities for growth and bonding.

But your journey doesn't end with the final page of this book. As you've seen, raising a puppy is a dynamic, ever-evolving process. As your puppy grows and learns, so too will your relationship. The key is to remain open, flexible, and responsive to your puppy's needs. Every dog is unique, and what works for one may not work for another. Trust your instincts, adapt the techniques as needed, and keep learning. Your puppy will be your greatest teacher, guiding you toward a deeper understanding of patience, empathy, and unconditional love.

As you move forward with your new knowledge, I encourage you to do so with confidence and dedication. The road ahead may have its bumps and curves. Still, with consistent practice and a heart full of love, you will see a transformation—not just in your puppy's behavior but in the very nature of your bond. You'll watch as your rambunctious little ball of fluff grows into a confident, well-mannered companion, ready to take on the world by your side.

And what a world it will be. With a well-trained puppy at your heel, every day becomes an adventure. Whether you're exploring new trails, visiting friends, or simply lounging at home, your puppy will be your constant companion, faithful friend, and partner in all of life's joys and sorrows. This is the promise of your journey—a lifelong relationship built on trust, respect, and unwavering love.

I want to leave you with a final thought as we part ways. The bond you forge with your puppy is a gift—a treasure to be cherished and nurtured. It's a relationship that will shape you as much as it shapes your dog, teaching you lessons of patience, presence, and the pure, simple joy of living in the moment. Embrace this gift with an open heart, and let it guide you toward a life filled with laughter, love, and the unending delights of a wagging tail.

And remember, you're not alone on this journey. As you implement the lessons from this book, I invite you to share your experiences with others. Join online communities, connect with fellow puppy owners, and let your stories inspire and encourage those just starting out. Together, we can create a world where every puppy is given the chance to become their best self and where every owner knows the incomparable joy of a well-loved dog.

May the bond you build be a testament to the extraordinary power of the human-canine connection, and may your days be filled with playful paws, belly rubs, and sloppy kisses.

We Hope You Enjoyed

Now that you have everything you need to raise a confident, well-behaved puppy, it's time to pass on your newfound knowledge and help other puppy parents start their journey with ease.

By sharing your honest opinion on Amazon, you're doing more than leaving a review—you're guiding another dog owner toward stress-free, positive training. Your experience could be the reason another puppy finds a happy, well-trained home.

Thank you for being part of this journey—your support means the world!

🐾 *Trinity Woods Press*

Leave a Review in Just One Click

Simply scan the QR code below or click this link to share your thoughts:

👉 https://www.amazon.com/review/review-your-purchases/?asin=B0F6YRXHZ5

Leave a Review

References

American Kennel Club. (n.d.). *New puppy checklist: Gear you'll need for your new dog.* American Kennel Club. Retrieved from https://www.akc.org/expert-advice/puppy-information/new-puppy-checklist/

American Kennel Club. (n.d.). *Puppy-proofing tips for your home and yard.* American Kennel Club. Retrieved from https://www.akc.org/expert-advice/puppy-information/puppy-proofing-tips-for-your-home-and-yard/

Madison Animal Care. (n.d.). *The importance of early veterinary visits for puppies and kittens.* Madison Animal Care. Retrieved from https://madisonanimalcare.com/the-importance-of-early-veterinary-visits-for-puppies-and-kittens

Ridgeside K9 NorCal. (n.d.). *Crate training made easy: Creating a safe space for your dog.* Ridgeside K9 NorCal. Retrieved from https://ridgesidek9norcal.com/crate-training-made-easy-creating-a-safe-space-for-your-dog/

American Kennel Club. (n.d.). *8 tips to help your new puppy adjust to a new home.* American Kennel Club. Retrieved from https://www.akc.org/expert-advice/training/8-tips-to-help-your-new-puppy-adjust-to-new-home/

Connor, E. (n.d.). *How to choose a name for your puppy.* Medium. Retrieved from https://connorethanblog.medium.com/how-to-choose-a-puppy-name-503c9931bb11

Connor, E. (n.d.). *How to help your puppy learn its name.* Medium. Retrieved from https://connorethanblog.medium.com/how-to-help-your-puppy-learn-its-name-6b7e8acf0c10

Dogster. (n.d.). *How to build trust with your dog: 8 vet-approved ways.* Dogster. Retrieved from https://www.dogster.com/dog-training/how-to-build-trust-with-your-dog

K9 Turbo Training. (n.d.). *Preventing separation anxiety in puppies.* K9 Turbo Training. Retrieved from https://k9turbotraining.com/preventing-separation-anxiety-in-puppies/

American Kennel Club. (n.d.). *Puppy potty training timeline and tips.* American Kennel Club. Retrieved from https://www.akc.org/expert-advice/training/potty-training-your-puppy-timeline-and-tips/

Doggie Lawn. (n.d.). *How to tell if a dog has to go potty.* Doggie Lawn. Retrieved from https://doggielawn.com/blogs/blog/how-to-tell-if-a-dog-has-to-go-potty

Sykesville Veterinary Clinic. (n.d.). *5 common puppy potty training problems (and how to address them)*. Sykesville Veterinary Clinic. Retrieved from https://sykesvillevetclinic.com/news/5-common-puppy-potting-training-problems-and-how-to-address-them/

Bond Vet. (n.d.). *Pee pads for puppies: The pros and cons*. Bond Vet. Retrieved from https://bondvet.com/b/puppy-pee-pads

Humane Society. (n.d.). *How to crate train your dog or puppy*. Humane Society. Retrieved from https://www.humanesociety.org/resources/crate-training-101

Pet Crates Direct. (n.d.). *The impact of puppy crate size on your pet's happiness*. Pet Crates Direct. Retrieved from https://www.petcratesdirect.com/blogs/news/puppy-crate-size-impact

American Kennel Club. (n.d.). *Positive reinforcement dog training: The science behind it*. American Kennel Club. Retrieved from https://www.akc.org/expert-advice/training/operant-conditioning-positive-reinforcement-dog-training/

American Kennel Club. (n.d.). *Separation anxiety in dogs: Signs, causes, and prevention*. American Kennel Club. Retrieved from https://www.akc.org/expert-advice/training/dog-separation-anxiety/

Best Friends Animal Society. (n.d.). *Food aggression and resource guarding in dogs*. Best Friends Animal Society. Retrieved from https://bestfriends.org/pet-care-resources/how-stop-food-aggression-and-resource-guarding-dogs

Hound's Lounge. (n.d.). *30 dog games to play with pups young and old, indoors and outdoors*. Hound's Lounge. Retrieved from https://www.houndslounge.com/blog/30-dog-games-to-play-with-pups/

VCA Hospitals. (n.d.). *Feeding times and frequency for your dog*. VCA Hospitals. Retrieved from https://vcahospitals.com/know-your-pet/feeding-times-and-frequency-for-your-dog

VCA Hospitals. (n.d.). *Feeding the mind and body: Interactive feeders for dogs and cats*. VCA Hospitals. Retrieved from https://vcahospitals.com/know-your-pet/feeding-the-mind-and-body-interactive-feeders-for-dogs-and-cats

American Kennel Club. (n.d.). *How to socialize a puppy*. American Kennel Club. Retrieved from https://www.akc.org/expert-advice/training/puppy-socialization/

Animal Humane Society. (n.d.). *Help your anxious or fearful dog gain confidence*. Animal Humane Society. Retrieved from https://www.animalhumanesociety.org/resource/help-your-anxious-or-fearful-dog-gain-confidence

American Kennel Club. (n.d.). *Come! Tips for training a reliable recall*. American Kennel Club. Retrieved from https://www.akc.org/expert-advice/training/reliable-recall-train-dogs-to-come-when-called/

American Kennel Club. (n.d.). *Want your dog to come when called? Play a game*. American Kennel Club. Retrieved from https://www.akc.org/expert-advice/training/dog-come-called-game/

American Kennel Club. (n.d.). *Finding and choosing the right dog collar for your dog*. American Kennel Club. Retrieved from https://www.akc.org/expert-advice/lifestyle/choosing-right-dog-collar/

Rover. (n.d.). *Introducing your puppy to the leash: A trainer's ultimate guide*. Rover. Retrieved from https://www.rover.com/blog/introducing-your-puppy-to-the-leash-a-trainers-ultimate-guide/

Preventive Vet. (n.d.). *Keep your dog training sessions short and sweet*. Preventive Vet. Retrieved from https://www.preventivevet.com/dogs/short-and-sweet-training-sessions

Psychology Today. (n.d.). *Ten tips to integrate dog training into everyday life*. Psychology Today. Retrieved from https://www.psychologytoday.com/us/blog/fellow-creatures/201912/ten-tips-to-integrate-dog-training-into-everyday-life

Pooch & Mutt. (n.d.). *High-value dog treats: The complete guide*. Pooch & Mutt. Retrieved from https://www.poochandmutt.co.uk/blogs/lifestyle/high-value-dog-treats-the-complete-guide

Printed in Dunstable, United Kingdom